SCALE
WITHOUT
FAIL

Grow Your Business
Successfully From
Pilot To Profit

Graeme Hosking

Scale Without Fail
Grow Your Business Successfully From Pilot To Profit

First published in Australia by Graeme Hosking 2021
www.pellucid.global

A catalogue record for this book is available from the National Library of Australia

ISBN: 978-0-6450568-0-8 (pbk)
ISBN: 978-0-6450568-1-5 (ebk)

Bookcover image: Jozsef Bagota © Shutterstock

Typesetting and design by Publicious Book Publishing
Published in collaboration with Publicious Book Publishing
www.publicious.com.au

This book is dedicated to William and Saskia, always in my thoughts

Note from the Author

In this book I have included a variety of charts and templates to illustrate my key points. If you would like to explore any of them in greater detail, please visit my website: www.pellucid.global.

Acknowledgements

Writing a book is a solo endeavour supported by many. This book wouldn't have reached its final form without the help of my book coach, Kath Walters, who helped me to tease out the main themes and structure them sensibly. Her approach for shaping a mass of ideas and stories also helped immensely in taking the fear out of the process — a great example of how timely advice can make a venture go better.

Thank you to my early chapter readers — Karina Kwan, Roger Church, Chris Power and Rita Newman for your feedback and comments. And thank you to Damian Johnson, Annie Le Cavalier and Louis Chien, who read the first version of the complete draft. Your individual observations and suggestions helped to make this a much better book.

Finally, a big thank you to Sara Carrillo for her editorial input and moral support throughout this project. It made all the difference.

Contents

Glossary

5Ps	The 5Ps framework groups every strategic consideration or constraint under one of 5 categories: Profit & loss, People, Process, Property, Paperwork.
80/20 Rule	80% of consequences come from 20% of the causes. Also known as the 'Pareto principle' and 'management by exception'.
Agile operations	Refers to a method for building technology faster than more traditional approaches.
Born global	A start-up (usually tech based) which needs to be global in scale to make business sense
ASIC	Australian Securities and Investments Commission
B2B	Business to business
BAU	Business as usual
CAC	Customer acquisition cost
CAU	Change as usual
CTB	Change the business
EVP	Employee Value Proposition — what the organisation offers its employees as a reason to work there; a key driver of attracting, engaging, and retaining talent.

GPM	Gross Profit Margin
GTM	Go-to-market strategy
HSE	Health, Safety & Environmental – regulatory requirements for business compliance
IP	Intellectual property
ISO	Abbreviation for the standards developed by the International Organization for Standardization. *ISO* is derived from the Greek word "isos", which means equal.
IT	Information technology
Johari window	A tool to help people understand themselves and their relationships with others. Its title combines their first names: Joseph Luft and Harrington Ingham.
KPI	Key performance indicator
Lean operations	Addresses waste and inefficiency in production, service and other process activities.
MBO	Management by Objectives, first formalised by management guru Peter Drucker in his 1954 book, *The Practice of Management*.
MBTI	Myers-Brigg Type Indicator. MBTI provides an indicator of personality out of 16 archetypes, based on 4 dimensions of how humans see and experience the world.

MIS	Management information system
MVP	Minimum viable product
P&L	Profit and loss
QA	Quality Assurance
R&D	Research and development
ROI	Return on investment
RTB	Run the business
ScaleCast	A living scale-up model upon which to build the business, and from which the finance team can also confirm the financial budget and cash-flow projections.
S-curve	Illustrates the different pace of the business as it goes from one "steady state" to -another, different "steady state" from Start, through Scale, to Stabilise.
SGS	Strengths, Gaps, and Style
Six Sigma	A quality method that seeks to minimise errors and quality variations in outputs of all kinds.
SME	Small and medium enterprises
SOAP	Strategy on a page
Steady state	Denotes the mature business, as fast growth slows down and the organisation settles into a different rhythm.

Strategy Compass	A powerful tool to work out your business strategy and make sure you've got everything you need for your ultimate state.
SWOT	Strengths, Weaknesses, Opportunities and Threats
TAM	Total addressable market
Vampire strategy	Where one business copies everything that another one does but aims to execute it better.
VC	Venture capitalist

Introduction

If you're a business founder or owner ready to grow your business, but you're not sure how, this book is for you. Your business may be profitable already, but you have bigger plans. Or it may be "born global" and need to be large to benefit from economies of scale to make money — think Uber, Xero, Square, Pinterest, Spotify, Tesla and almost every new payment or foreign exchange business.

- You need this book if you:
- know you need to grow, and grow fast
- know you need a plan, because you haven't done this before
- have done this before but know you could have done it better.

Not Business as Usual

Let's face up to an uncomfortable truth: scaling up a business is different from starting a business. Most scale-up initiatives fail because of poor execution, *not because they are a bad idea*. The saying: "fail to plan, plan to fail" is very relevant to these businesses.

By "scaling up", I am talking about two things: building a business with many more employees than you can get around a conference (or dining room) table; and building a business where the pace of growth is very fast, with the first stage of peak growth usually occurring over one to two years. This is not to say you can't run a successful, profitable business that grows steadily larger. But that's a different business challenge that plays out over a much longer timeframe.

To succeed in a fast, high-growth scale-up, you must understand the prize and the effort required to achieve it. With these two essentials clear in your mind, you can shape your approach to achieving success.

In this book my aim is to provide a simple guide through the key points you need to consider, and to show you how to deal with the most common problems you may encounter in scaling up your business. This is not intended to be a detailed guide to project or change management. If you need or want more detail, I recommend you read through this framework as a first step, to give you a solid foundation from which to explore further.

Why Should You Read This Book?

If you're ready to grow, you're probably both excited and worried. You're looking forward to the challenge, but you know the stakes are high. If you're looking to scale up your business, there'll be so much for you to deal with on a day-to-day basis that it will be easy to become distracted.

It may seem like a luxury to read a book about the steps you need to take to scale up successfully. But if you don't, it might feel as if you are crossing a new continent with no idea of where you're going. As Burke and Wills[1] found when trying to cross Australia, that may not end well!

You may have a lot of experience in business, but unless you've already grown businesses and run them at scale, you'll make mistakes along the way — we all do. Fast growth is so different from organic: it's scary and painful. Mistakes get magnified.

When you're learning to ski, as I did many years ago, you start slowly on a gentle slope and everything is fine. Then you get onto a steeper slope and your speed picks up. You feel that you are going down the hill too fast, and you fall over at your first turn because your technique is not yet good enough. As my first instructor helpfully said (after I'd fallen over), "Every fall begins with a turn"!

---

1. In 1860, Robert Burke and William Wills led an expedition over 3,000 kilometres from Melbourne to the north coast of Australia. They both died without making it back, as did all but one of their expedition.

The speed and steepness of the slope amplify everything — good and bad. Good technique learned from experience and clear instruction is the only solution. It's also true with the rapid pace of change in a scale-up. To succeed, it's not enough to be stronger, work harder, or even slow things down so you can cope better. In a scaled-up enterprise, your end state will be a business that is radically different from what you have now.

Think about the metamorphosis that a caterpillar goes through to become a butterfly. Within the cocoon, the change process means that the caterpillar digests itself, and then creates the butterfly from the raw materials. It's painful and literally all-consuming. That's a good way of thinking about transformational change. It's a bigger deal than most people think. Getting a guide — a simple step-by-step roadmap — that gives you a picture of where the change will take you is something that anyone starting to scale up should find essential.

Why Did I Write This Book?

After a career building big teams in major banks, I took that leadership experience into the world of scale-ups, where I soon realised that many of the founders and other small-business owners I dealt with had never worked in a bigger business, and so weren't always clear on how to get there. Or even where "there" was.

Many of the things within this book I've learned the hard way through my own mistakes. It's the 80/20 Rule.[2] But the 20% you do pay attention to, you have to get right. I've included frameworks and tools you can use that work in practice, not just in theory. I've included the steps I've taken to build scale-ups that have got to their targets, while also paying attention to things that leaders need to do to avoid the chance of failure.

I based this book on my experience, both as a mentor to, and as a leader of, scale-ups. The tools that proved to be useful, I have

---

2. Also known as the 'Pareto principle', after the 19th century economist Vilfredo Pareto who observed that in many outcomes 80% of consequences come from 20% of the causes.

included here. The others, I have ditched. I will walk you through many of the questions that came to me as I went through my own scale-up journeys, and I will pick out the most useful answers I've found.

The Scale without Fail Approach – A 7-Step Roadmap

Over the course of this book we will work through a seven-step process, which covers the things you need to get right if you want your scale-up to succeed.

Because this book is all about you (the reader) leading change, the first step starts with you, and what the change required by your scale-up means to you.

We'll then look at the other most important elements for successful execution in a scale-up, grouped into 5 key topics:

- Execution Strategy & Plan
- Cash (Financials)
- People (Team)
- Stakeholders
- Risks & risk management.

We'll finish by describing what your business should look like as you get to full-scale – your **Arrival** point. Something for you and your team to aim at as you build your business during the scale-up.

Throughout, we'll follow the guiding principle that scale-up leaders need to keep everyone's attention focused on the same critical success factors. I have found the best approach to build a scale-up includes:

- Simple goals (not complex spreadsheets or lengthy business plans)
- Management by exception (the 80/20 Rule)
- Measure what matters (describing expected outcomes through key progress metrics).

You can see what we'll cover summarised in the roadmap graphic below.

Step 1	Step 2	Step 3	Step 4	Step 5	Step 6	Step 7

You & Change	Strategy	Financials	People	Stakeholders	Risk Management	Arrival

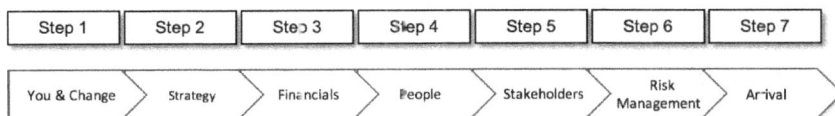

The Scale without Fail Approach: A 7-Step Roadmap

Why Adopt This Approach?

One thing you can guarantee in a scale-up: nothing will go exactly to plan! Every scale-up has a lot of moving parts. All of them need management attention when change is at full tilt. So it's helpful if you have already identified what's most important, together with simple guiding principles to keep the scale-up on the right track.

Keeping this framework simple, rather than a long shopping list of things to consider, or a "PowerPoint manual" of a change plan, makes it easier to implement the key points into your real-life scale-up in practice.

During my career I've managed a lot of large change-management initiatives, including scale-ups. I've also helped others through their own growth programs. What I've found is that, under pressure, *most people default to the simpler approaches rather than the more sophisticated.*

Of course, sometimes businesses need more sophisticated techniques. For example, you may need to adopt Six Sigma[3] process-improvement methods if you are optimising quality, reliability or efficiency in a standard process.

But, in general, what business leaders need is what I call "guard rails for common sense". In other words, frameworks that keep the scale-up on the right path but don't divert lots of management effort into approaches that may distract leadership attention from what's truly important.

---

3. Six Sigma is a set of techniques and tools widely used for process measurement and improvement, first introduced by American engineer Bill Smith while working at Motorola in 1986. https://en.wikipedia.org/wiki/Six_Sigma

What About Funding the Scale-Up?

As you go through this book you will notice that we don't spend much time on the subject of raising capital to finance your scale-up. We *will* talk a lot about the financials of the scale-up, but not how to get the money to fund it. This is deliberate.

Many scale-up leaders spend much of their time focused on pitching investors for money, working out valuations, and planning eventual investor exits once the business has reached its valuation goals. While it's important to get these right, especially in technology scale-ups, I've often seen too much attention given to raising capital and not enough given to how that capital is going to be used for maximum benefit.

This book is about building your business well and will help you answer the usual first question from any investor: "What are you going to use the money for?".

For readers looking for an overview of fundraising topics, as well as more details on the areas covered in this book, I have included further resources on my website: www.pellucid.global.

What's Next?

Your success is important — not just to you and your business, but to all the staff, customers and suppliers who depend on your success. The driver of this change must be you, the leader. Time after time, we see unprepared leaders fail, and well-prepared ones triumph.
So we'll look at the scale-up process in three parts:

1. You — and what you're aiming for.
2. Scale-up basics on how to build and manage growth.
3. The business at scale – when it has reached your initial growth targets.

This book gives you a snapshot of the whole scale-up from start to finish, as well as concrete and specific steps to take. It will give you the confidence to set out on your scale-up journey knowing that you will nail it. You will be the best scale-up leader you can be, as you learn how to *scale without fail*.

CHAPTER 1
Change Is a Choice

Australia has numerous small businesses — more than 2 million enterprises with less than 20 employees. However, many small businesses don't create (or sustain) enough economic value for their owners. Nearly one-third — 600,000 — of Australian small businesses earn annual revenues of less than $50,000.[4] That's just about one person's average Australian annual income. It's a living but not a great one — a "low value trap", which many small businesses find hard to escape from.

Over any normal three-year period, two-thirds of small businesses launched in Australia either fail or only reach break-even. These numbers tell us that breaking out of this "low value trap" is hard.

What is going wrong? In my experience, if you scale up without a well thought-through approach, you will struggle to get where you want to be. Even if you succeed, it won't be without a lot of wasted effort. And you may run out of cash before you get there.

If you are not used to running a business with a structured approach, you may be uncomfortable with some of the tools, templates and guidelines proposed to help you scale up successfully. But if you set aside that bias, *you will succeed.*

Judgement is the key thing. This book will help you focus on the most important things, so you can do the minimum needed to be safe

---

4. *Australian Government. Australian Small Business: Key Statistics and Analysis,* 2012, p. 7. https://treasury.gov.au/sites/default/files/2019-03/AustralianSmallBusinessKeyStatisticsAndAnalysis.pdf

and successful without getting distracted by "nice to have" solutions that will not failure-proof your growth plan.

It doesn't have to be as hard as the statistics might suggest.

"Scale-up coaching" is a well-established segment of the business advice profession. I'd like to acknowledge, for example, Verne Harnish and his 2014 book *Scaling Up: How a Few Companies Make It ... and Why the Rest Don't.* Scale-up coaching has become a successful growth industry of its own! That is reassuring to see, as I have been a business mentor, and still am. It's work I love.

But the sheer volume of advice on offer can confuse, and sometimes overwhelm. Scale-up leaders often seem to conclude it's too hard or not relevant to them, and so decide to set off with no proper guide. In this book, my aim is to take you through the scale-up journey using as much of a structured approach as is relevant — *and as little of it as is possible.* I believe we should follow the advice often attributed to Albert Einstein: "Everything should be made as simple as possible, but not simpler".

Let's Talk about You

Before we get into the details of scaling up, we need to look at where you are starting from, and what that implies for the business change you want to drive.

You may think you are already clear on your current position and know what you want to achieve, and all you need to learn is the tools to scale up. Well, bear with me. So many times I've found we look outwards for answers when we should start by looking inward. It's a good idea to check in with yourself and your core team. You want to be certain of starting from the right place, and with the right attitude. This is a good time to confirm that your core assumptions are correct and built on solid foundations.

Many influential leaders, thinkers, and writers make this point. "Be the change you want to see in the world" is a quotation often attributed to Mahatma Gandhi. Whether he said it or not, he certainly acted it out when he led a peaceful revolution that secured independence for the world's largest democracy, India, after hundreds of years of British rule.

You may not be trying to do something as ambitious as freeing a subcontinent. But often significant change is only successful because of the personal commitment of the person driving that change. A change leader understands that achieving change starts with a change in their own behaviour.

Framing the Problem (Hint: It's an Opportunity)

Science tells us[5] that there are only small physiological differences between fear and excitement. In both cases your heart races, your skin gets clammy, your breathing accelerates. But there's an enormous difference between them in terms of how they make you feel, and your resulting capacity to act. *So how you frame the nature of growth is an important step in your future success.* Something that inspires excitement in some people may well inspire fear in others!

The first point to make is that speeding up your business growth is not about changing your business alone. It's about changing everything connected to it, including your work team, your stakeholders — and most important of all, yourself.

Many research studies show how our perception of the world differs *depending on our perspective*. Renowned psychologist Daniel Kahneman[6] won a Nobel Prize for his lifetime study of this issue, which Michael Lewis described in his 2016 book, *The Undoing Project*. Kahneman showed how when you frame a situation differently, people make different decisions, even when the situation itself is the same.

This suggests you will automatically reduce your chances of success in any endeavour if you have the wrong perspective. *You need to make your mental frame of reference as accurate as possible to achieve your goals.*

Most people will view your scale-up differently, depending on their

---

5. "Predictable Fear", *Psychology Today* https://www.psychologytoday.com/us/blog/prefrontal-nudity/201410/predictable-fear

6. "The Framing of Decisions and the Psychology of Choice", by Daniel Kahneman and Amos Tversky, *Science*, 1981.

role. Not everyone is excited by change, or how it feels to go *through* change. So understanding what others think about your plans, and how your plans will affect them, is an important foundation for your success.

When I started in business, I thought everyone would be as excited about change as I was. I was certain that once I had explained our mission, it would be simple to get on with the plan. I soon discovered how wrong I was, after my first few projects didn't go to plan.

Some people don't like change, and it takes more communication, detailed discussion and plan development before they can fully support it. To reach them, you will need to work hard to clearly define your goals and milestones. I'm not talking detailed plans here; I mean something you can explain easily (preferably without slides!). You want to avoid lofty mission statements, in favour of concrete statements of what you will do, when and how.

This doesn't mean you, as the scale-up leader, have to become an amateur psychologist. But it's important for the leader to check in with everyone critical to the change (including yourself) on how they feel about it, and how they see it unfolding. *You will be surprised at the pain points and misconceptions that emerge.*

Anyone preparing themselves for change can expect to feel some trepidation. If they don't, it means either the change isn't very significant, or that they haven't thought through the full impact of the change. Repeatedly, I have found that one of the most valuable things in leading change is to accept that uncomfortable feeling, and to realise that it's normal. If you have an obvious goal, and logical ideas on how to get there, you can manage your discomfort as you go. The rest of this book will give you tools and hints to help you get there.

You — the Driver of Change

The title of Marshall Goldsmith's great 2007 book *What Got You Here Won't Get You There* highlights the main issue for most business leaders or owners looking to make a significant change in their business. The skills and aptitudes you have leveraged to get your business to this point are very different from the ones you will need to change your business at pace, and to run it.

We will cover the main practical points you should consider later in this book. But first you need to understand your role as the driver of change. We can boil this down to 3 key questions:

1. How ready and willing are you to change?
2. Do you understand your role as a change agent?
3. Do you understand your motivation for this change and the effort/results trade-off?

In the rest of this chapter we'll step through these three questions and then look at the nature of the scale-up change itself.

How Ready Are You To Change Yourself?

It's difficult for us to change ourselves — even small habits can take a long time to break. Ask anyone who has tried to go on a diet, get fit, or stop smoking. But if we want major change to happen in our business, it's unlikely to happen without a similar major change occurring in the way we manage that business.

How many times have you seen leaders who expect others to change, but themselves to stay the same? I've seen a lot of it, which usually doesn't end well. Humans are good at spotting inconsistencies and react cynically when they see them: like the political leader who travels by private jet to give a lecture on limiting climate change. If we are leading change, we have to set an example of the business we want to change towards — and manage the pressures that the process of change will bring.

When you consider your own motivations and responses to significant change, it will help you make the right trade-off between running your business better as it is (e.g. through improving sales margins and reducing overheads) or setting out on a major scale-up journey.

If you want more income, or an increase in the future sale value of the business, but don't want everything to change by much, *then a scale-up may not be the best choice for you*.

Understand Yourself

When you begin a journey, it's important to know your starting point. For driving business change, <u>you</u> are the starting point so it's important that you've thought about yourself, and how well-positioned you are for the change you want to lead.

There are many tools available for assessing personality and capability.[7] If you have had the pleasure of completing a self-assessment at some point, you will know they help you answer the key question: *How well do I know myself?* Good self-knowledge will make you better prepared for everything that scale-up change will throw at you.

What self-assessment doesn't answer is the follow-on question: *How well do others know me?* In your scale-up you will rely on others for their support, hard work and advice, whether from friends, family, colleagues or advisors. But the value of that support will depend on the frame of reference they have about you, and the challenges you are facing. It's a framing issue once again.

Others may assume you know certain things, or want to achieve certain things, when the reality is different.

Likewise, you need to be careful not to assume that "it worked for them, so it must work for me". One way of avoiding this potential mismatch of reality versus perception is to consider the "Johari window" framework *(see Figure 1.1)*. This tool was created 65 years ago by two psychologists[8] to help people understand themselves and their relationships with others (its title combines their first names).

Most people spend their emotional and business lives focused on the left-hand side of the grid. But the greatest value is sharing with others what <u>you</u> don't know about yourself, but <u>they</u> do (your "Blind

7. Best known is the Myers-Brigg Type Indicator, or MBTI, now over 70 years old. MBTI provides an indicator of personality out of 16 archetypes, based on 4 dimensions of how humans see and experience the world.
8. Joseph Luft and Harrington Ingham. See https://en.wikipedia.org/wiki/Johari_window

Spot"). Or things <u>they</u> don't know about you, but which are true and relevant to how you do things (your "Façade").[9]

You may not want to go through a formal exercise using the Johari window or something similar with your team or stakeholders. However, it is a useful framework for reviewing how you interact and communicate with others, and your readiness for the change you are leading. The better you understand these elements, the more effective you will be in leading change.

Johari Window

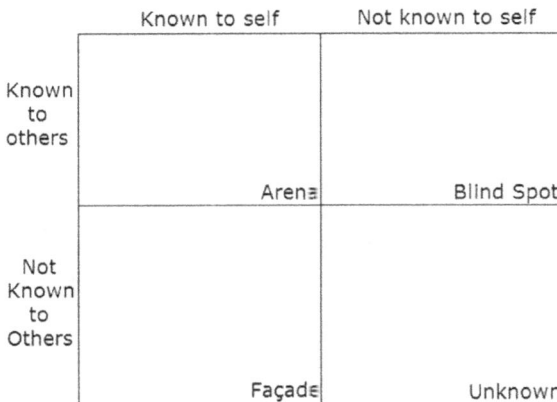

	Known to self	Not known to self
Known to others	Arena	Blind Spot
Not Known to Others	Façade	Unknown

Figure 1.1: The Johari Window

What's Your Motivation?

Your motivation to grow your business may be based on the idea that "growth is good, and extreme growth must be extremely good"! But this thinking may lead you astray.

A focus on growth for its own sake can drive you onto what psychologists call "the hedonic treadmill". No, it's not a new form of get-fit-quick misery. Hedonic means pleasure, and in this case, pleasure arising from material achievements or possessions.

9. Therapists may need to help you fully understand the "Unknown" quadrant, equating to your subconscious.

It's a well-documented aspect of human psychology that many of us try to achieve more happiness through gaining more in our lives (money, possessions, power). But as we gain more, we adapt to our current state, so we need more and more things (more money, possessions, power) to keep happy. After a while it feels like we are on a treadmill, or perhaps a hamster wheel, running as fast as we can to gain more, to feel happier.

If you are scaling up because it appears to be the obvious next step for you on the treadmill, take care! *(See Figure 1.2.)*

Figure 1.2: Hedonic Treadmill

Although many small businesses make little money, many are what management consultants Hoffmann and Finkel[10] call "owner-led" businesses, which can provide a great lifestyle for the owner even if they are not growing much over time.

It's wrong to assume that every "owner-led" business is right for a scale-up exercise. If the owner wants to create a more valuable business, then growing larger may involve more personal challenge than the owner is prepared for.

---

10. *Scale: Seven Proven Principles to Grow Your Business and Get Your Life Back*, by Jeff Hoffman and David Finkel, 2014.

Sometimes the right answer is not to scale-up, but to make sure the business is getting the best margins from the current revenues. This can improve bottom-line profits without changing the size or nature of the business and how it needs to operate.

It all depends on your motivation for growing your business, as seen in "The Story of the Mexican Fisherman", which I summarise below:[11]

An investment banker visiting a small Mexican village sees a small boat laden with fish. He gets talking to the owner and asks how many fish he has caught. The owner replies: "Only enough to support my family's immediate needs." The banker then asks, "But what do you do with the rest of your time?"

The Mexican fisherman says, "I sleep late, fish a little, play with my children, take siestas with my wife, stroll into the village each evening where I sip wine and play guitar with my amigos. I have a full and busy life."

The banker offers to help him: if the fisherman spends more time fishing, he will lend him the money to buy a bigger boat. With the proceeds from the bigger boat, the fisherman can buy enough boats eventually to have a fleet. Over the next 15–20 years he would make so much money he could leave the village and move to a big city, launch an IPO, sell company stock to the public and become very rich.

"But then what?" asks the Mexican. The banker replies: "Then you would retire. Move to a small coastal fishing village where you would sleep late, fish a little, play with your kids, take siestas with your wife, and stroll to the village in the evenings where you could sip wine and play your guitar with your amigos."

---

11. Author unknown. The full version can be found on Courtney Carver's blog https://bemorewithless.com/the-story-of-the-mexican-fisherman/

Putting It All Together

This isn't a psychological profile of the core characteristics of a successful scale-up leader. I don't believe there is only one kind of person who can lead a scale-up. But you should get to know yourself as well as you can <u>before</u> you launch your change.

Think of it this way: if your job was creating spreadsheets, you would expect that a better knowledge of the spreadsheet program should help you deliver a better spreadsheet, developed in less time and with fewer errors.

<u>You</u> are one of the most important "tools" you have to effect change. So you should seek to understand how well-placed you are to lead the change you are considering.

No-one wants you to go through the upheaval and risk of changing your business without knowing why you are doing it. You need to know upfront what personal changes you are prepared to make, and how you will manage differently after your business has been transformed.

CHECKLIST: YOUR PERSONAL STARTING POINT

Consider (and answer for yourself) the following key questions:

- What are your personal goals in making this change?
- What will you need to change in your approach to achieve this goal?
- What help do you think you will need and what areas will be the most challenging for you in making the change needed?
- Are you committed to growth — or is there another way to achieve your goals?

Self-scrutiny can be daunting. It might seem self-indulgent — but it's not. It's the basis for you getting everyone, including yourself, lined up and ready for the change. A leader who considers the personal aspects of this change is easier to follow than one who does not. Let's now talk about that change.

The Nature of Scale-Up Change: Introducing the S-Curve

Everyone has had exposure to change in their life, starting with their own growth from babyhood to adulthood. In most businesses today, change has become a constant. For many businesses, it's no longer BAU (business as usual) but CAU (change as usual).

However, the degree of change implied in a rapid scale up of a business requires a very different approach from managing smaller, continuous change. The S-curve *(see Figure 1.3)* illustrates the different pace of the business as it goes from one "steady state" to another, different "steady state". It's important to recognise the difference in these states — and the pace of change — in order not to get caught out by the differences.

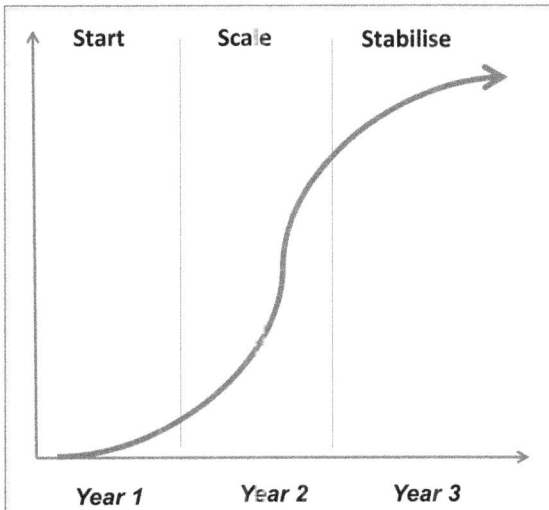

Figure 1.3: The S-curve of Change

If you try to manage a business through major change as if BAU, that change is likely to fail. The energy and determination needed to make major change happen is different from what is needed to manage steady-state business. This is especially true of the end state, when your business reaches the intended target size and performance level. It will be much larger than before, so it will suit neither the old "BAU" way of managing, nor the "fast growth" that got it to this new scale.

The human brain finds it very hard to conceive of — and so manage — periods of extreme change. We've seen this in the exponential growth in pandemic infection rates, which outstrips the responses based on more normal "linear thinking".

A great illustration of this principle is the fable "The Wheat and the Chessboard":

> It is said that the inventor of chess, Sessa, requested that his reward from a grateful ruler should be a grain of wheat for the first square on the chessboard, and then double that for every square, up to the total of 64 (the number of squares on a chessboard). The ruler laughed it off at first as a meagre prize for such a brilliant invention, only to have his treasurers explain to him that this would amount to over 18 thousand million billion grains (18 with 18 noughts after it). It's about 1.2 trillion metric tonnes of wheat, or over 1,500 times the global production of wheat in 2019. Such is the power of exponential growth!

Most business change rarely ends up as dramatic as this — normally, the exponential change curve flattens out, even in pandemics. But significant growth rates quickly change the management challenge for the business leader, which will not be obvious in the "BAU" phase of the S-curve.

I've seen many people that can manage change and BAU — *but rarely well at the same time.* That's why larger organisations usually have separate BAU and Change leadership teams.

Change v Steady State

A series of changes can occur over a longer period. But rather than being an elongated S-curve, a better way to consider this is as a series of interlinked S-curves, with periods of stability, in-between faster periods of change. *(See Figure 1.4.)*

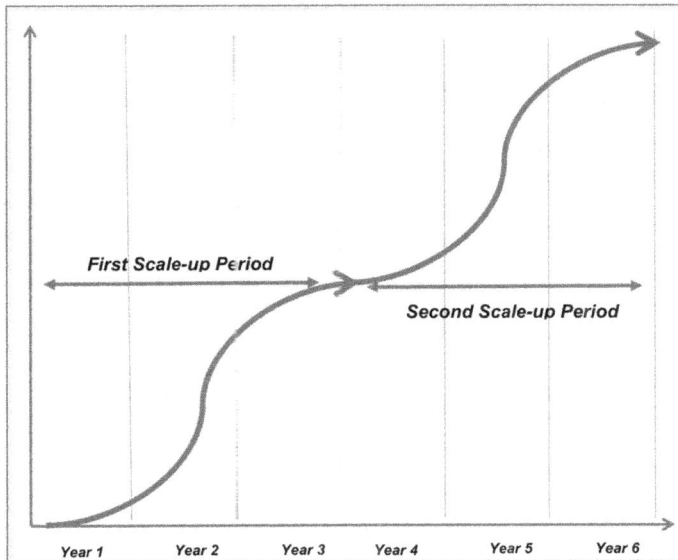

Figure 1.4: Interlinked S-curves

This is how evolutionary change occurs in nature, through a process known as "punctuated evolution". Long periods of little change are followed by episodes of quick change over a relatively brief period. Animals that thrive through this period of change are often different from those that lived in the earlier stable period. *(See Figure 1.5.)*

Figure 1.5: Dinosaurs in Denial

Change management is a large and diverse topic, founded on project-management disciplines. Although detailed project management is not the focus of this book, we'll cover the principles important to managing your scale-up as we proceed.

CHECKLIST: TAKEAWAYS FOR THE SCALE-UP LEADER

- **Think through your motivation, and your concerns** — what you want to achieve in building a scale-up business, and also, what your key questions or concerns are in getting to the top of the S-curve.

- **Consider the expected duration and scale of the change period** — the steep part of the S-curve.

- **Plan for the differences between change and BAU**: You will need different people, processes, metrics, and messaging through the period of change, compared to the steady-state business.

- **Be clear about your goals**: Change starts with you, the business leader, and major change requires a different approach than BAU.

Next Steps

Now we have checked the starting point for your scale-up journey, we need to be sure you are heading in the right direction. And to confirm your direction, you need the Strategy Compass we'll look at in the next two chapters.

CHAPTER 2
The Strategy Compass – Demand and Supply

An old saying goes that, when picking fruit, make sure before you climb the ladder that it is leaning against the right tree. Similarly, when building a business, you should first be sure you are aiming at the right end goal. Many businesses that start with a growth plan focus on the immediate next steps, rather than on where they're going and what they're aiming for. This causes genuine problems.

Solving this challenge is not about creating a beautifully worded vision or mission statement. For example, saying "We want to be the world's biggest X" doesn't give you a clear idea about the steps needed to achieve that goal. It states your business aspiration of where you want to be, but these statements often are more inspirational than practical. What's needed is something to bridge the gap between an aspirational goal, and the practical steps to reach that goal.

To help bridge this gap, I've developed a framework, which I call the "Strategy Compass". You can use it to organise all of your scale-up thinking around a set of concrete, significant, and energising goals. It's a powerful tool to work out your business model and make sure you've got everything you need for your ultimate state.

Every significant scale-up journey will be both stressful and rewarding. So before you start, it's a good idea to find out whether your goal is viable. A big change like a scale-up is challenging because it is very different from your current experience, and so *it's not always easy to know if it is going where you want it to go.*

It's tempting to skip this step if you think you know the answers already. But if you do skip it, you may miss some things that are crucial to your longer-term success. The Strategy Compass will help you test the viability of your goal before you commit time and effort to your venture.

I've used the compass both formally and informally. I've taught it to others, who have found it useful in testing the viability of their business. It's not rocket science. It's loosely adapted from the "Five Forces" Michael Porter wrote about in his famous book from the 1980s, *Competitive Advantage*.

The framework will help you look at your business from the outside in and summarise the major elements of success. By doing this, you'll ensure that you have considered all the main points needed in your scale-up, and that you are heading in the right direction. That's why it's called a "compass": strategy at its simplest is about making firm choices on the direction in which you are taking your business.

The Strategy Compass Framework

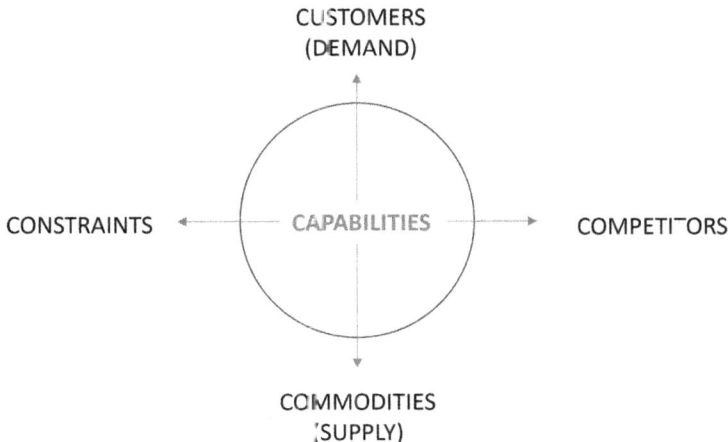

CUSTOMERS
(DEMAND)

CONSTRAINTS ← CAPABILITIES → COMPETITORS

COMMODITIES
(SUPPLY)

Figure 2.1: The Strategy Compass

As you might expect, there are four points to the Strategy Compass framework, with the main north-south axis describing the ***demand and supply*** ("pull") dynamic that will drive your growth, and the east-west axis covering the other forces ("push") in the environment that you are operating in.

- North: Customers (Demand)
- South: Suppliers (Supply)
- East: Competitors (Environment)
- West: Constraints (Environment)

We'll step through each location on the compass, and then summarise the key questions you should be able to answer in each area in the form of a checklist. This will help you confirm the viability and direction of your scale-up and highlight the areas where you need to develop better answers.

Let's start by looking at the crucial driver of the business, the demand and supply axis, before we move onto the rest of the compass in the next chapter.

True North — Customers

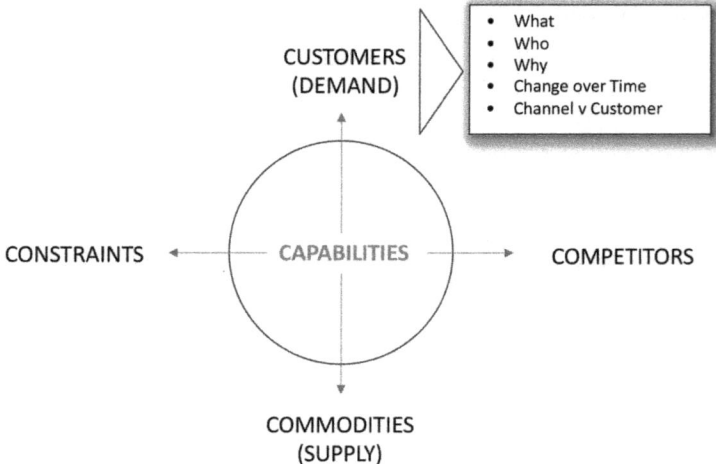

Figure 2.2: Strategy Compass — Customers

It is an unfortunate truth, only occasionally acknowledged, that there are many business solutions out there looking for a problem! What seems like a "neat" idea to the business owner, to the potential customers may not appear to solve their problems at all.

This first compass point is intended to confirm the reality of the demand for your scale-up. It shows you've clearly identified your customers and their needs, and *realistically assessed* their willingness to pay you for meeting those needs, at levels where you can make a profit. From this, you can confirm that your solution can scale up to meet that demand. Your solution may be a brilliant idea, but sometimes a successful small idea doesn't turn into a successful large idea. We want to be sure that the problem is big and painful enough for consumers or customers to want to pay for your solution.

Without customers, there is no business. You may have customers already, but sometimes your business doesn't have a deep understanding of who those customers are, nor what their needs are (or will be) as you grow. *You cannot assume they will come with you as you scale up*.

Let's look at customers (current and future) through answering three questions: **What** is the size of the market? **Who** are these customers? **Why** are they likely to buy your offering?

Step 1: What Size Is Your Potential Customer Base?

One of the first questions asked by venture capitalists (VCs), and other folk looking at the potential of growth businesses, is: *What is your total addressable market (TAM)?*

Your answer to this question has to consider the growth prospects of your scale-up, based on a combination of facts and estimates. These usually combine **demographic data** (how many target buyers, in which geographic market), with estimates of **purchasing intention** (percentage of buyers likely to buy), and **price assumptions** (perceived value of the solution being offered). What comes out of these high-level analyses usually sounds very concrete, and also large — for example, "$40 billion, 2 million potential customers".

Any appearance of certainty is unfortunately a dangerous illusion. Your ability to confirm these assumptions is what successful scaling up is all about — as is your ability to capture even a fraction of the TAM at reasonable levels of risk.

Defining your TAM tells you how big your opportunity is, and leads on to the next key question: *Who are the specific buyers in this TAM?*

Step 2: Who Are Your Customers?

This might seem a simple question, but it's a big one. There is a whole industry devoted to answering it. Marketing experts often talk about customer "personas". These describe the ideal or target customer for the business. They provide a summary biography for the business' "ideal" or representative target customer.

Persona summaries usually include the target customer's age range, occupation, education, and personality. They also summarise the customer's psychology: motivations, goals, frustrations, and attitude to technology. These "pen portraits" give the business a deeper understanding of buyer behaviours and motivations and can be very helpful in developing product features or service solutions that meet their needs more accurately.

If your business is technology-based, it's highly likely that you will have developed personas for it, as this is now fairly standard practice in IT and online channel businesses. However, if you have target customers identified in this way, there are two further points to consider: Crossing the chasm and Not confusing "channel with "customer".

EXAMPLE

Name:	Fred Founder			

DEMOGRAPHICS		**VALUES & GOALS**	
AGE	38	PERSONALITY	Extrovert, Big Picture, High energy
GENDER	Male	WORK GOALS	Launch, build and float business in 3–5 years
FAMILY STATUS	Married		
LOCATION	SYDNEY	PERSONAL GOALS	Keep fit, retire at 45, surfing
INCOME	$100,000		
EDUCATION	BA COMMERCE	**CHALLENGES & PAIN POINTS**	
WORK		PAIN POINTS	*IT scale up; team management; investors*
INDUSTRY	Finance/Fintech	FRUSTRATIONS	Hard to find the right staff fast; so many business elements need urgent attention
COMPANY	ZupaClick (online start-up)		
JOB TITLE	CEO & Founder	AFRAID OF?	People headaches – Hiring the wrong people; running out of cash; slow growth
TECHNOLOGY INFLUENCES		**Problem Statement**	
PERSONAL	Latest smartphone, Mac	"I want to build a fintech business quickly, and need trustworthy advice on what I should do to be successful"	
MEDIA	Twitter, Instagram, WhatsApp		

Figure 2.3: Customer persona

Crossing the chasm

Personas should describe the future (scaled-up) business, *not the one you are running today.*

Many fintechs and other businesses get capital and get started without fully understanding and defining their customers. This leads to some confusion, and it's hard to know what's needed to identify, attract, onboard and keep paying customers. Many of the businesses I talk to are at that stage where they've started, got to a certain stage and then realised, "We don't know how to get the customers on board in sufficient numbers. We've made an assumption that has turned out to be off the mark."

Early customers who come on board are often different from those you want at scale. This difference between the needs and buying behaviours of your first customers ("early adopters") and the mass market ("pragmatists") is described in Geoffrey A. Moore's excellent book *Crossing the Chasm: Marketing and Selling High-Tech Products to Mainstream Customers*, which I highly recommend.

So your current customers are unlike your future customers. This was the case in the smartphone market: the first adopters were most interested in having a new technology that was exciting and sexy. The later adopters, the mass market, only bought when they could see that the product was reliable, functional and easy to use, and also reasonably priced. That's a very different market for the smartphone providers to scale into.

You see variations of this adoption cycle as every new technology emerges, and then moves into the mass market. The chasm that Geoffrey Moore describes is the transition needed to get your product or service from the early adopters, who are often the geeks who like new stuff, to the rest of us who say, "I just want something that does the job well".

What appeals to the early adopter is usually not what drives buyers in the mass market. If you don't differentiate these "buyer personas" and consider the new or changed features that your service or product needs, it's highly likely your scale-up will struggle to generate the pace of demand and growth you want.

I had my personal experience of this change in buying behaviour when I launched the first online banking service in the UK. In the mid-1990s we had dial-up modems, and it was a big chore for users to get online. The kind of customers we first brought on board were high-net-worth people. They were time-poor but wanted visibility of their finances and liked extra features like money-management software. So we built links into several of the most popular software programs of the day — and charged a fee for it.

However, as we rolled out the service into the wider market, we found that people wanted something different. For them, it was about simplicity and lowest cost, not about financial analytical capabilities. We developed a fresh approach and pricing structure for this mass market, and eventually found that the cost of supporting the extra features wanted by the early adopters did not justify further investment, compared with the needs of the entire market.

If we had stuck by the "persona" of our initial customers, we would have reduced the speed and success of our roll-out enormously.

Not confusing "channel" with "customer"

Many scale-ups rely on other businesses to sell their product to the end customer. We often refer to these intermediary businesses as a "channel" (as in, channel to market), or as a strategic partner.

A common example would be an accounting firm that offers an accounting software package (like MYOB or Xero) to its customers. In this case, the accountant is a channel to the end customer for the software provider. This makes the accountant's customer also the end customer of the software provider.

The complication is that what your channel partner likes about your product or service may not be the same as what the end customer values, and vice versa. So you may want to develop a persona (or profile) for the channel partner as well as your end customer.

One scale-up I worked with had to deliver a great claims repair service to an insurer's customers. What the end customer cared about was the reliability and quality of the repair, and the speed of response to the initial claim. The insurer's top priorities were different: they really wanted to see lower repair cost, faster speed to complete, and excellent workplace safety behaviour.

Without being able to show that it could meet these "channel" partner needs, the scale-up would have never had the opportunity in the first place to deliver services to their end customers.

Channel partners can accelerate sales growth for smaller businesses. Looking at it another way, consider which channel you can reach your end customer through. There are many channels through which you can buy Xero, for example, but some are more likely than others to generate end-customer confidence and sales.

Your scale-up needs to show your channel partners that there is enough value to make it worth their while to distribute or sell your product.

I worked with one scale-up that assumed banks and tele-communication service providers would distribute its software, but these channel partners didn't think it was important enough to prioritise in their marketing campaigns. This lack of interest meant that the scale-up plan had to be drastically redrawn in order to re-focus on a direct marketing campaign. You can imagine how different the scale-up timeframe, logistics and marketing would be between these different channels to market.

Step 3: Why Would Customers Buy Your Product?

The persona-led marketing approach helps a business identify its target customer. But knowing who you want to sell to is just the first part of the puzzle. Knowing <u>why</u> they would buy, and why from <u>you</u>, is the key next step. This may be an obvious point, but I am constantly struck by how few business leaders can easily explain "why do they want it, and why from <u>us</u>?".

Different types of customers (early adopters, pragmatists) have different reasons to buy the same product or service. However, all of them will decide whether your offering is valuable enough for them to buy, and whether you are a reliable provider.

Sometimes the channel partner being used can provide that perception of good value and trustworthiness. Hence the success of third-party online sales through Amazon. Customers trust Amazon to deliver what they have ordered, even if they don't know the brand of the product provider at first.

If your target customer cannot easily work out the extra value provided by you, compared to the alternatives, then this will flatten your scale-up growth trajectory. This is why so many businesses try to drive sales through setting a price point, then offering a discounted deal.

For business to business (B2B) sales, the scale-up business may want to refer to relevant case studies where previous satisfied buyers have seen reduced cost, less effort, or greater returns from using the product or service.

My advice is to *be as concrete as possible*. The reason we see so many social media posts that include a number ("5 reasons to read this book") is because human beings respond positively to numerical evidence. We feel we can judge the value more easily where it is a number, not a qualitative statement.

This also explains why so many online marketers will refer to the $ cost of alternative services or software bundles, against which their offering looks like very good value. If your potential customers are comparing your offering with something that they consider to be of similar or higher value at a lower cost, it is hard to achieve scale-up traction.

It's important to ensure your target customers compare your service with the alternatives you want them to compare it to. So if you're selling cyber insurance, for example, you compare the cost to "only one cup of coffee daily", not "several times the cost of Netflix per week". *Same amount, different reference point*. This **anchoring** of your price to a flattering comparison can make an enormous difference to the success of your proposition.

The Moving Target

Throughout your scale-up journey you will learn more about your customers, and your channel partners. That's normal, and helpful. Some of that additional information will help you adjust your aim as you move "across the chasm" into the mass market. Some of it will correct fallacies and gaps in understanding that even experienced marketers may hold about your target customers.

I have found that to be the case in the scale-ups I have led. It seems reasonable that if you are doing something as novel as a scale-up, then you will along the way learn additional things that challenge some widely held beliefs.

As we work our way around the Strategy Compass, expect that you will need to update your assumptions and goals repeatedly. To be truly valuable, we should see the compass as a work in progress, with regular iterations and amendments as we learn more. For this reason, expect that the detail behind your description of your customers will change (and deepen) over time, especially as you move into execution of the scale-up.

Completing Your Compass Customer Checklist

Many readers may already have completed more detailed go-to-market reviews. You should use this framework as (1) a checklist for your customer/market strategy, to ensure you have not overlooked a key element or assumption; and (2) a summary of the customer or market need that you think your scale-up will satisfy.

The level of detail you go to in this exercise is up to you. As a minimum you should look to answer the *What, Who,* and *Why* questions.

1. **What** is your TAM? (We'll look at market sizing in the next chapter.)
   - Size (numbers, $ revenues)
   - Geography
   - Growth of market (% pa)
   - Expected market penetration/conversion (% over 3–5 years)
   - Gross Profit Margin expected (% of TAM revenues)

POINTS TO WATCH OUT FOR:

- *Confusing market size with market opportunity*: For example, there may be 2.3 million SMEs (small and medium enterprises) in Australia, but they're well spread geographically, and not always easy to reach. And 1.5 million of them have less than 20 staff, with net earnings for the whole business less than the average Australian wage, about $50,000. It's a big market numerically but many of the individual customers may not be worth chasing.

- *Overstating expected conversion rates*: How much of your TAM is genuinely likely to be interested in and available to your product? Be realistic on how long it takes to bring customers on board.

- *Overstating your Gross Profit Margin (GPM) or considering it as net profit*: GPM provides a better view of the value of the scale-up opportunity than sales revenue alone. It shows you the underlying returns from the business once you have completed ramping it up. However, it doesn't include all the scale-up costs, like IT build. (Hint: if you don't know the GPM percentage this should be a red flag for your scale-up.)

2. **Who is your customer:** Describe your target customer.
   - Build a simple persona (*see example in Figure 2.3 above*).
   - Identify how this persona changes as you move into the mass market.
   - Identify channels to access this market (the go-to-market strategy, or GTM).
   - Create a channel profile (persona) if this is an important part of your GTM.

POINTS TO WATCH OUT FOR:

- *You may have multiple personas*: However, you should try to keep this simple. Creating different personas for the end customer as opposed to your channel partner (or customer) may be useful, where they have different needs or priorities. If you end up with more than 5 personas, consider whether you are aiming at too many target customer segments.

- *Document your initial GTM assumptions:* How are you going to connect with your customers, engage them and convince them to get them on board? How much will go through channel partners? How much online? Mail shots? A calling campaign? All of these channels have different economics, timescales and conversion rates, which your plan should consider.

- *Check your customer acquisition cost (CAC) assumptions are realistic*: You will need to assume that your CAC will change as you scale. You may need to offer different features or levels of service (e.g. a larger in-house helpdesk for less IT-literate customers). Your TAM/CAC should include expectations around retention and customer churn, as these can have a big impact on execution capability and costs, as well as customer satisfaction.

3. **Why should your customer buy from you?** Describe the Value Proposition.
   - What needs does your product/service meet ("there's a specific need").
   - Price versus value provided ("it's worth it").
   - Why better than competitors/market alternatives ("us not them").

POINTS TO WATCH OUT FOR:

- *Is the "customer need" enough to spur customers to action?* As most businesspeople have observed, customers don't always act logically. For example, many will spend money on betting on events with a very low chance of winning, but then not want to spend any money on insuring themselves or their property against damage or loss, something with a much higher chance of occurring. If your scale-up is satisfying a "new" need, or a complex one (like insurance), check that you can (a) explain it clearly, and (b) the customer's motivation to solve that need is sufficient to make them buy.

- *Check that you know who the final decision-maker on the purchase is* If you are selling to a company or other organisation, it's likely that more than one person will make the ultimate purchase decision, based on a range of features. Let's assume you're a provider of world-class PC screen wet wipes, for example — you may be the best solution for the end users in the company, but unless the procuring managers see your product as the best value, lowest-cost, and most ethically sourced, you may not get selected. You need not solve all these problems at this stage, but you should know them to factor in a realistic % customer conversion rate, or level of CAC.

Is All This Really Necessary?

You'll see from this section that it can be hard work to build a detailed understanding of your customers, even for the purpose of market-sizing. Some business leaders decide this is just too hard. They would prefer to take their brilliant idea, build a prototype and see how it goes. This is where the concept of "minimum viable product" (MVP) comes from: get something that can be quickly and (relatively) cheaply put into the market and then revise it with customer feedback as you go.

While that approach may work for some technology start-ups, it can be a much slower and more "learn-from-our-mistakes" way to grow. Scaling-up a business at speed (without first running out of money) needs a robust scale-up plan. A critical first step in building that plan is to be as specific as possible about your customer, and their propensity to buy from you.

Now that we've considered the demand side of your scale-up business model, let's look at how (and from where) you meet that demand: the supply side.

South — Suppliers

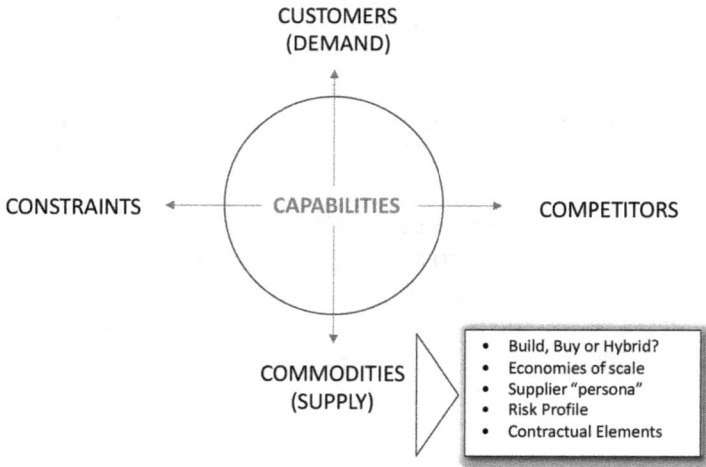

Figure 2.4: Strategy Compass — Suppliers

Once you know what your market (your customers) want, you need to be sure you can supply what's needed, at the quantity, cost and quality required. Understanding the supply side of your business strategy is a key part of building your scale-up plan.

Even where you are selling services that you may supply mostly yourself — your expertise, or your software — there will always be elements that third parties need to provide when you are at scale, like handling customer service calls.

Your detailed execution plans will need to consider more standard procurement questions, like writing and negotiating supply contracts. For now, your focus in th s Strategy Compass section should be on the **critical** features of your supply strategy — those that have the biggest impact on your scale-up **pace, effort** and **cost**.

Often a clear understanding of your supply strategy can make the difference between success and failure.

In the 1990s, I worked for one of the largest credit card companies in the world — Barclaycard in the UK. They built an online shopping mall in the early days of the internet, to offer attractive products to their millions of card customers, making commission from the extra online sales turnover.

But they couldn't get enough stores in the system, and as a result card customers weren't interested in coming to the online site — which then made it less interesting for major retail brands to build an online store in the Barclaycard mall, a classic "chicken and egg" problem.

The moral to this story: be sure your proposition considers the supply-side dynamics as well as the demand. If your suppliers cannot support your innovative ideas, your scale-up will be a hard slog.

Some business models only make sense at large scale. Some of the biggest new market players — Uber, Amazon, WeWork — are all businesses that rely on very large scale and high shares of their target markets. Now imagine a scaled-down taxi firm. They cannot compete on price with Uber, which can spread its cost of building and managing that business across tens of millions of services.

Understanding the source (and scale) of supply for your scale-up is important, and especially so if your business model assumes large scale to work in economic terms.

Product v Service Scale-up

Before we look at your supply strategy, let's note that this will differ depending on whether you are selling a (physical) product or a service (such as software, or professional advice).

If you're a product business, potentially importing raw materials or finished products from overseas suppliers, there are some specific points you need to be clear on.

- Whatever the type of product you are buying — raw, processed or fully manufactured — consider whether your supplier gives you more than just the lowest-priced product. Many businesses have found that a **lengthy supply chain** can expose them to logistics problems and costs they had not planned for. A shipping delay can drive down profit, or even risk losing business, disappointing customers who may not come back.

- **Reliable quality** can be worth more than the lowest price. For example, one business I knew was sourcing herbal tea from Nepal, an attractive product with a fast-growing customer base in Australia. The major challenge was ensuring product quality from the small overseas producers. If you're importing products, it's critical to ensure your supplier can always meet the local Australian regulations on quality in the sourcing and packaging of what you are bringing into the country to sell.

- The **terms of trade** (time to pay) that suppliers offer you can have a major impact on your working capital. It can significantly affect your ability to scale up economically. One import business I know has built a very positive relationship with their overseas suppliers over many years. As a result they have achieved generous trading terms (90 days credit or more), which frees up capital to invest in other costs, like marketing, and expanding the business.

- Despite the value of a supportive lead supplier, **diversifying your sources of supply** when you are going well is the best approach, so unexpected events do not derail you. Businesses that rely on a few suppliers can get caught out if that supplier has a problem. Like a fire at their factory (it happens), or even a shutdown caused by extreme weather (monsoons in India), or a pandemic which closed many suppliers in China that were relied on by Australian businesses. Challenges ike this can significantly set you back.

Supplier Scale-Up Strategy

Many businesses **outsource** their administrative work — accounting, legal, secretarial, IT support services — and this may be an effective way of reducing the administrative load for early-stage scale-up businesses.

A key strategic question for both product and service scale-ups is how much of their **core service offering** they build in-house or through outsource providers.

- *Build:* If you want to do everything in-house, how will you find all the people you need? How will you onboard, train and induct them to the level of quality needed, promptly and at the right cost for you? This was a key factor in the insurance claim repair scale-up I ran, with an enormous impact on the roll-out plan.
- *Buy:* If you prefer a more virtual service provider, are you comfortable with the economies of scale? Take the example of Rev.com, a transcribing service. You send them your audio recording; they transcribe it for a certain fee and then send it back. It's a variable cost model, and at a certain volume it becomes more expensive to do externally than hiring someone to do it internally.

- *Hybrid:* There is nothing wrong with starting "virtual" or outsourced and then bringing functions in house as you grow. Just remember that setting up these service functions takes much longer than you think it will, especially if all or most of the knowledge on how to run the function sits with the outsource provider, and not inside your business.

To help you decide how you should organise your scale-up, there are plenty of "build v buy" business models that might help your thinking. Probably the best known of these is the "core v context" model from Geoffrey Moore. In a nutshell, it says you should focus on building the things that create most value for your business and your customers and offload those processes that are least valuable or least differentiating. For example, if you need warehousing for your product, you may find that an external warehousing specialist provider (whose core business is managing warehouses) would manage this better for you than you would by hiring a warehouse manager or doing it yourself. Their core business is your non-core (i.e. your "context") function.

It makes excellent sense to only do things that add most value but be sure that your chosen supplier can scale with you. Look at the case of Zoom, the video business that went from 10 million to 200 million users in early 2020 at the start of the coronavirus pandemic. As a 10-million-user provider, they were fantastic. But 200 million users brought questions about security and quality, particularly in the corporate market.

One major lesson I learned the hard way during my career is that you should *never outsource a problem and expect it to go away*. Even if a supplier can provide a service for lower cost and better quality than you can do internally, remember that you will still have to manage the supplier proactively. At some point you will need someone on your team (if not you) who is responsible for ensuring that the supplier delivers what you need and can keep doing so as you scale-up.

Bigger businesses see professional supplier management as an important area of focus, where they can make large cost savings. As a scale-up, your success wil depend less on lowest costs and more on the broader considerations that drive your supplier strategy. For example, if you are selling into larger businesses, they will usually demand certain minimum requirements from their suppliers (e.g. you) — but also from your own supply chain.

One major corporate customer of a scale-up I was leading required me to warrant (formally) that none of my suppliers was engaged in modern slavery (i.e. under-paying their workers), and it is common to require quality standards like ISO 9001 or security standards like ISO 27001 from suppliers. In this scenario, it's better to consider this requirement upfront, before you outsource your IT build to a small team of offshore developers, where you have no certainty over what and how they are doing your work.

CHECKLIST: YOUR SUPPLY STRATEGY

1. Based on your scale-up's Customer Strategy Compass, summarise the key services or products you need to supply. Separate internal functions (admin, support) from business delivery. For example:

   Internal Functions

   - Accounting (including Finance, Payroll)
   - Legal
   - Payments Handling & Processing
   - Premises (Security, Servicing)
   - IT Support (desktop, servers, web hosting etc.)

- HR & Staff Recruitment
- Marketing (including SEO, online and social media management)
- Logistics (warehousing, delivery)

External (service) functions

- Customer Sales
- Customer Service
- Product or Service Supply
- Service Delivery (if not part of supply)
- IT Build (apps, core platform)

2. For each function, decide whether you plan to make or buy (outsource) the supply capability.

3. Flag those functions where you think economies of scale mean that you should start them outsourced and then bring them in-house at scale.

4. For the outsourced functions: build a brief description of your supplier. Think of it as the counterpart to your customer persona. It should be clear enough to share with a third party so that they will be able to find you a supplier. It should include anything you consider relevant to support your scale-up business. (See Table 2.1 below for examples.)

5. Finally, consider the risk profile of your suppliers. Summarise the functions or suppliers where you see the most risk, based on your scale-up plans and their inherent nature. We'll talk about how you address these risks in your scale-up execution plans, later in this book.

Table 2.1: Supplier Dimensions

Features	Examples of key contractual questions

• Location (e.g. country. Does it have to be Australia? Are any countries excluded?)
 	
• Corporate status: (e.g. Pty or not?)
 	
• Share of business: Sole supplier (100% provider) or targeted share of business (say: at least 10% but no more than 25% of turnover)
 	
• Required compliance with standards. Such as:
 	
  ○ ISO 9001 (quality)
 	
  ○ ISO 14001 (outsourcing)
 	
  ○ ISO 27001 (information security)
 	
  ○ Australian Data Privacy standards
 	
  ○ Australian Health & Safety regulations
 	
  ○ Australian industry-specific standards (as needed by your industry/offerings)
	• Terms (e.g. 30 days+ on invoice)?
	
	• Expected level of annual business? (Note that every supplier will normally limit their \$ exposure to individual customers, especially ones that are growing fast.)
	
	• Length of contract (12 months to 5 years)?
	
	• Price, and triggers to renegotiation (e.g. annual increases limited to CPI, volume discounts)?
	
	• Warranties (e.g. 5 years for manufactured products or installed services)?
	
	• Exclusivity (for them selling to your competitors in your market, or you to sell overseas)?

Bringing It All Together

When you start your scale-up journey, you may not be clear on everything that you need from all of your suppliers. As always, this Strategy Compass exercise is designed to highlight the areas where you most need to build better answers, and where you are likely to face the biggest challenges to the delivery of your scale-up.

For functions where you don't have a clear idea on your supply options, I suggest you make the best guess you can, knowing that you will revisit these assumptions as you make progress with your plans.

The key thing is to reduce your level of uncertainty, and to highlight the areas where you need to do further work. So it's okay to say: "I can't answer any questions here, I will need to look at this again."

Summary — Demand and Supply Axis

Now that you have completed the first two sections of the Strategy Compass, you will have documented the core of your business: the demand that your scale-up is going to serve, and the sources of supply that will allow you to meet that demand. I see these as the "pull" elements of your business strategy, lifting your business to greater scale.

Like anything simple in concept but complex in practice, getting this far may be tougher than you expected once you get into the specifics.

My advice is: *don't get bogged down in the details*. But <u>do</u> complete the customer and supplier profiles in whatever detail you can, with special attention to the areas where you feel there is least known (by you), and where there is the most potential impact on your scale-up.

What's Next?

Now that you've got a good summary of your growth engine, in the next chapter we'll complete the Strategy Compass by looking at the factors that might **push** your strategy in the wrong direction.

CHAPTER 3
The Strategy Compass – Push Factors

In the last chapter we looked at the main engine of the business: the **demand** in the marketplace your scale-up will tap into, and the sources from which your business will **supply** that demand. Now it's time to look at the other strategic factors that will affect your scale-up.

In the East-West axis of the Strategy Compass we'll cover the forces that will have a big say in the success of your plan: what your **competitors** are doing, and what other constraints (external and internal) you may find in executing your scale-up strategy.

Why bother looking at these points now? Well, think of your scale-up strategy as a **push/pull** model. "Every action leads to an equal and opposite reaction" as Sir Isaac Newton's Third Law of Motion says, and it applies to business as much as it does physics. Customer demand will **pull** your business into greater scale; the strategic forces axis will naturally **push** back on this growth, unless you manage it well.

Let's start with the most obvious question: who are your competitors and what are they doing that may affect your scale-up? (And if it's such a great idea, why aren't they already doing it?)

East — Competitors

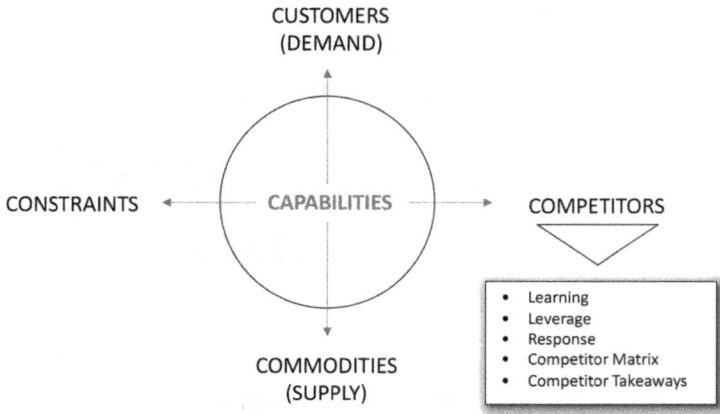

Figure 3.1: Strategy Compass— Competitors

It is a rare business that doesn't have competition. Even where new scale-ups have created an alternative business model, competitors are soon nipping at their heels. Think of Uber, which has seen Lyft, Hola, and dozens of other new ride-hailing businesses rise up in its wake.

If there is no visible competition, you should be asking yourself whether the market opportunity is really there. Or whether everyone is "staying out of the water" because a bigger business is about to launch into your sector and take it over. Remember web browsers in the early days of the internet? Netscape led the sector in the 1990s, but Microsoft's Internet Explorer then dominated. (Ironically, the latter has now been superseded by Chrome and Safari, so even the big fish can get eaten by bigger competition in a later round.)

Some scale-ups appear to have the mindset: "Build it and they will come". But this only works in the movies.[12] If you build a business, and customers are coming to it, there will be a competitor building a similar business nearby.

---

12. From the 1989 movie *Field of Dreams*: "Build it and he will come". A saying sometimes used in business to justify building something to generate demand from users, when that demand may not be obvious in the current market.

The Value of Competition

The good news is that competitors aren't just a problem for your scale-up to overcome. They also represent an enormous opportunity. First to learn, and second to leverage. If they are likely to respond in harmful ways (such as dropping their prices, reducing the margins you can charge), you need to understand whether this will cause a major issue for your scale-up strategy.

Let's look at these three points in more detail: learning, leveraging and responding.

1. Learning

It's always good when we learn from our mistakes. But it can be less painful and expensive to learn from the mistakes of others.

If you examine what others are doing in your target marketplace, how they tackle the customer base you're focused on, and how they position themselves in the market, you will gain insight into many important aspects of how _your_ business can capture the same opportunities. Competitors can help you see where the value is, and what works in the marketplace. You can use your competitors as a way of shortening your own period of learning.

In the insurance claim repair scale-up I led, there were several major competitors, all of them using the same way of doing things, the same operating model. This gave us a baseline: it was easier to see the minimum qualifications and capabilities required to be competitive. It also "set the scene". Unlike some new businesses, we didn't have to explain what we were doing or why to the customer (in this case: the insurer). We could focus on doing the same things (insurance claim assessment and repair) better, at lower cost. Our new operating model allowed us to fix the biggest bugbears for our customers, using the traditional way of doing things.

If you are coming into a market to disrupt it — which is what most scale-ups say they want to do — it can be tempting to ignore the current incumbents. "Oh, they are the old way of doing things, they don't get it," you might think. But this leaves so much low-cost learning on the table. I have found most times that the leaders of scale-ups find it hard to describe their competitors, or how their new proposition stands up against these existing players. But any executive hearing a pitch from a potential provider or partner company will always ask (often as their first question): "Who else does this? Who does this for us now? How do they compare (price, quality, customer outcomes)?". I know when I was in senior operational roles at various banks, I always wanted to get that perspective.

My advice is: don't ignore your competitors. Learn from them. Describe your competitive proposition in the ways your customer cares about. If you can, use external reference material to show your customers how well you're positioned against your competitors.

2. Leveraging

Sometimes you can do more than learning from your competitors' activities in your chosen market. You can leverage their experience directly.

The most obvious example of this comes in the form of experienced staff. I'm talking about open advertising for roles you need, so it's all legitimate. But if your scale-up business model is bringing something new to the industry, then there are likely to be good people working for your competitors who are already thinking, "There's got to be a better way to do this". Sometimes you will be approached by good staff who want a change, or a better place to work.

Interviewing these experienced people will give you useful information on what works and doesn't work in the marketplace. Hiring experienced staff can help you turbo-charge your scale-up, if you pick the right people. But be careful not to hire a majority of staff from just one firm — you don't want to recreate the culture and approach of your competitors (I've seen this happen).

The action point here is: don't focus only on your competitors as companies; instead, look at the skill sets and capabilities of the key staff that may be useful to you.

Sometimes, you may find that a competitor can be a source of work in the early days of your scale-up. This applies where you are entering a market with subcontracting as a feature (e.g. tradie work, building and construction). Although not a classic approach for a fast scale-up, doing work for other market players while you build your team and capability is a good way to "play yourself into the market".

One other approach is worthy of mention. It's what I call the "vampire strategy". This is where one business copies everything that another one does but aims to execute it better.

Tech start-ups are often fearful of someone else "stealing their great idea" and building it before they can. It's why patents and non-disclosure agreements (NDAs) are a big focus in these businesses. Most competitive advantage — even in tech businesses — comes less from the *strength of the idea* and more from the *quality of the execution*.

Twenty years ago I saw this close-up, with a UK traditional shirt manufacturer that made and sold high-quality business shirts. For decades they had been sending out catalogues and accepting mail orders, then posting out the shirts to their customers. It was a successful but slow-growing business that over time had built up a reasonably sized market for mail-order business shirts.

Their business model was copied by two consultants who had come along and seen an enormous opportunity. The interlopers took their own catalogue online and were much better at marketing, quickly building more marketplace presence than their competitors. They picked off the original company's customers, who liked the new convenient way of ordering. Within three years they dominated the market to the point where the original shirt manufacturer struggled to stay in business.

Superior execution can be a valid scale-up strategy, without a radical new technology or business model. You should consider whether a competitor could execute your model better. If so, then you need to have contingency plans for managing that threat before it becomes a reality.

This leads us into a more traditional competitor consideration: dealing with competitor activity.

3. Responding

You should always expect competitors to respond aggressively to a new or fast-growing business, even if their response is not obvious at first.

Consider whether competitors are likely to respond through **price** (dropping their costs), **value** (giving better quality or more of the product or service), or by raising **barriers to entry**. Barriers to entry might range from poaching your key staff to casting doubts on your operational reputation. The latter occurs mainly in a B2B environment, where the main customer decision-makers are a few key executives who can be briefed quietly on the issues with your quality, reliability or regulatory compliance.

If you are a tech business, you need to assume that larger technology businesses will move to exploit the opportunity you have identified. "Fast follower" responses from Microsoft, Apple, Google and others have taken over existing niches and flattened entire sectors. Think of the online translation market, now that Google Translate is available free on every smartphone.

Leveraging market presence can be the other way that leading brand competitors can threaten your scale-up. There have been high-profile examples where the best technology has lost out to the stronger market player. Remember the "videotape wars" in the 1980s, where Sony's superior Betamax format lost out to JVC's more popular VHS format? One might make similar claims for the way Microsoft used its marketing clout to pull users across from WordPerfect (to MS Word) and Lotus 123 (to Excel) in the 1990s.

Your competitors' response will change depending on the stage of your scale-up. It might change from ignoring you when you are in the Start stage of the S-curve, to creating barriers to entry while you are growing (Scale stage). When you are at scale, the competition will probably focus on price, value, and marketing clout.

You may also see that most sincere form of flattery, **imitation**, as competitors raise their game and copy parts of your operating model where they can do so easily. If you are executing well, don't worry.

Toyota has been showing people (including competitors) around its factory lines for decades, but still outperforms everyone in efficiently making cars at scale.

If your competitors copy you, think of this as a wholehearted endorsement of your approach, and focus on executing your model as well as possible. When other companies want to play the game your way, then it's good news — you should back yourself to win a game that you have invented!

The "Black Swan" Competitor

When European travellers first arrived in Australia, they found to their amazement that the swans here were black, something they had never seen before, which was why everyone had assumed all swans were white. "Black Swan" is what we now call an event that no one has expected. You could say that COVID-19 is a "black swan" event. Although the world has seen pandemics before, it's been at least a century since any have had such a global impact.

When you're thinking about your strategy, recognise that a "black swan" competitor may blindside you, just as Sony was blindsided when Apple's iPod launched in 2001.

For over 20 years the Sony Walkman defined listening to music on the move, building a massive share of the global consumer music market. By the late 1990s, new competitors based on MP3 technology had fragmented that market, but neither Sony nor its competitors predicted that a struggling computer manufacturer could dominate the market within just a few years of entry. In the 7 years after launch, the iPod captured 50% of the US player market, while its nearest competitor had less than 10%. Sony meanwhile fell into loss that same year and did not make a profit for another 7 years.

Let's hope your scale-up is the "black swan" for someone else! Meanwhile, working out where you are vulnerable to competition is a valuable exercise. It will come in handy as you consider your scale-up risks (which we'll discuss in more detail in Chapter 8).

CHECKLIST: BUILDING YOUR COMPETITOR STRATEGY

- List **the major competitors** in your target market. Keep this limited to the top 5–10 companies.

- Look at the basis on which they compete — price, value (features, quality offered).

- Plot them on a simple 2x2 chart (see *Figure 3.2, next page*), placing your scale-up against these features, based on your own view to start with.

- Use this Competitor Matrix to test the **competitive strength of your proposition** with trusted industry experts, potential channel partners, and potential customers: **update it with their feedback**.

- **Rank your competitors**, based on your perception of who are the market leaders ($, and best practice, if different)

- Identify any key **learning points** you might want from each competitor (if none, highlight the mistakes they make that you want to avoid)

- Consider **leverage opportunities**: staff, subcontracting, business model lessons. Find any key staff in the industry you want to target.

- Consider likely **competitor response** to your market entry: this may differ by stage of your scale-up. You should record your thinking in a simple Competitor Response template. (*See Table 3.1.*)

- Summarise any key **competitor takeaways** from your thinking: highlight any areas of potential concern in aspects of your scale-up approach compared to the competition or their likely response. This can be high level, but as you build your scale-up execution plan in more detail, focus on things you can action. (*See Table 3.2.*)

Table 3.1: Competitor Analysis Matrix —Summary Example

Stage	Competitor Response by Type			
	$	Quality	Features	Other
1. Start	X	X	X	Ask about your plans
2. Scale	10% GPM reduction	Advertising on experience of competitor team	Focus on gaps in your offering v established players	Negative PR re scale-up
3. Stabilise	15% GPM reduction	Hire new QA team	Bundle & sell with other services	Active poaching of your staff

Table 3.2: Competitor Takeaways — Example

Topic	Comments & Observations
Channel partners	Will be targeted on health & safety, quality concerns (via negative PR): need to build good management information systems (MIS) to show performance (proof points).
Competitor A	Has good technology but average management. Good source of team leaders but need to ensure strong cultural training during induction & onboarding.
Competitor B	Likely to compete aggressively on price. Quality not good. Prioritise the marketing messaging needed by us.
Price reaction	Potential margin squeeze of ~10% when at scale. Factor into our execution and financial plans.

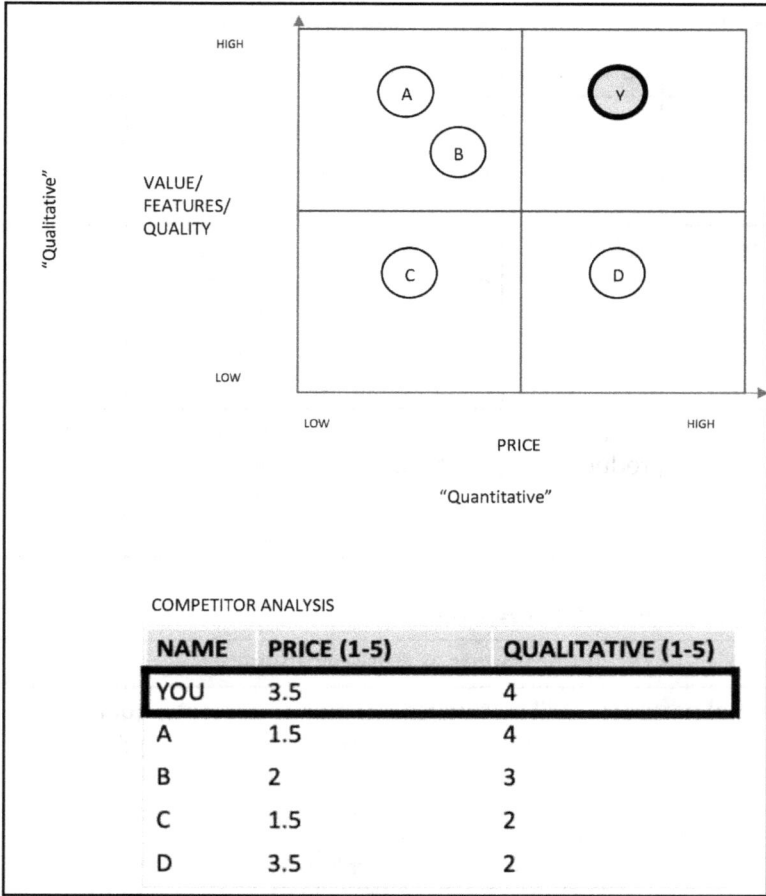

COMPETITOR ANALYSIS

NAME	PRICE (1-5)	QUALITATIVE (1-5)
YOU	3.5	4
A	1.5	4
B	2	3
C	1.5	2
D	3.5	2

Figure 3.2: Competitor Analysis Matrix

Is This Necessary?

It's possible that as you start your scale-up you don't have a complete view of your competitors; perhaps it is a fragmented industry without identifiable market leaders. Or you may believe you are creating a totally new market, so you have no direct competitor. In which case you may think: "I don't see the value of spending time on competitors".

I have come across early-stage scale-ups who say this, and my answer is: are you sure?

Take a look at how Coca-Cola viewed their market opportunity when they had over 50% of the global fizzy drink market. They considered that they were competing against more than just Pepsi and other coke companies. They saw their competition as being every kind of drink that consumers might consider as an alternative to Coke! Tea, coffee — and even bottled water. This thinking led them to enter many other drinks market segments, and to position Coca-Cola against the broader consumer demand for leisure drinks, not just current coke drinkers.

If you do nothing else, consider this: what alternative to my scale-up offering is my customer considering, and why? And, given this, what do I need to do to make them choose my business instead?

West — Constraints

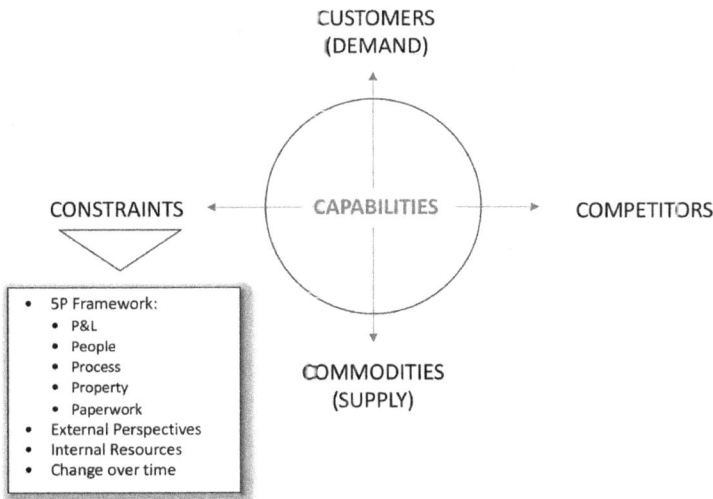

Figure 3.3: Strategy Compass — Constraints

By prevailing over all obstacles and distractions, one may unfailingly arrive at his chosen goal or destination. – Christopher Columbus (1451–1506)

The last part of the Strategy Compass should summarise the factors that might hold back your scale-up strategy. It's a useful discipline to consider these upfront, because it forces you to focus both yourself and your team on the things that need most attention. It is an approach of cautious optimism, summed up in the saying: *Aim for the best, but plan for the worst.*

Looking at constraints tells you how much effort and time are needed to manage these challenges. If I had known beforehand how long it would take my team to negotiate contracts with third-party suppliers, hire the right people, get the licences needed to do business, and lodge effective patents, I would have managed several scale-ups differently in my career!

It's true that constraints to growth can differ across different businesses (and leaders). But common themes affect most scale-up businesses, and in my experience it's helpful for every scale-up to consider these themes, and to work out those most relevant to them.

SWOT or Not?

You might have already identified many issues via a SWOT exercise. This is a standard tool many businesses use, where they identify their strengths, weaknesses, opportunities and threats (hence, SWOT). Review your "weaknesses" or "threats": these are the constraints to consider in your execution planning.

If you have already completed a SWOT exercise, look through the checklist at the end of this section, to check for issues you have not fully considered. There are three reasons to do so:

1. **Viability:** Identifying constraints allows you to confirm there are no insurmountable obstacles to your scale-up strategy.

2. **Execution Planning:** You will identify key activities you need to build into your execution plan, to avoid delays to your scale-up.
3. **Risk Management:** You will have a starting list of potential risks for your later management and reporting processes (as we cover in Chapter 8). This may also help support your case as you look for external funding. Investors look for leaders who understand how to defend their market.

Identifying Your Constraints

The quality of output from SWOT exercises can be very uneven. If you do a SWOT analysis the traditional way — getting your team around a whiteboard in a workshop and throwing out ideas — then the issues identified can range from the very specific to the very general, with little differentiation. You can end up with a list that goes from "not enough car parking" to "how do we get regulatory licences in every Australian state?".

You don't want a shopping list of random things to discuss. Remember the 80/20 Rule: you should be looking for the top issues that will have a <u>material</u> impact on your scale-up. They might be *gaps in business capability* — which will take time, money or effort to remedy. There may also be *marketplace challenges* that you need to take into account — such as increasing regulatory pressure (e.g. in financial services), negative media perceptions (e.g. towards multi-level marketing schemes), or logistical challenges (e.g. finding and using offshore suppliers during a pandemic).

Strategic constraints are important enough that you need to manage them right from the start. My rule of thumb is to limit the list to a maximum of 10 issues. If you track more at this stage, you will get sucked into execution planning rather than strategy validation, which is not the purpose of the Strategy Compass exercise.

To help you keep focused, I suggest you look at these challenges through the lens of a simple framework that I call "the 5Ps".

The 5Ps Constraints Framework

The 5Ps framework groups every constraint under one of 5 categories, namely: profit & loss, people, process, property, paperwork. Within these broad categories you can see more examples of the detailed constraints your scale-up might want to consider.

- **Profit & Loss:**
  - ○ ***Revenue model:*** is your sales conversion proven/do you have sales capability?
  - ○ ***Funding:*** do you have enough/have you factored in delays in getting revenue?
- **People:**
  - ○ ***Leadership*** — *Experience? Objectives from the scale-up (clear, aligned?)*
  - ○ ***Skilled staff*** — *Identified? Available? Time to onboard?*
- **Process:**
  - ○ ***Operating Model****: Clear progress from MVP/pilot to full production?*
  - ○ ***Complexity****: How easy will it be to train your staff/ partners/customers?*
  - ○ ***Scale performance****: Are your processes fit for volume, variations and exceptions?*
- **Property:**
  - ○ ***Intellectual Property (IP)****: Do you need/have patents? What's your approach?*
  - ○ ***Footprint:*** *do you need office/warehouse/sales space? Time to source/secure?*

- **Paperwork:**
  - ○ ***Regulatory:*** Licences needed (by state)? Regulatory approval needed (e.g. ASIC, TGA[13])
  - ○ ***Customer/Contractual requirements:*** ISO, Data Security, IS Security, Quality, HSE[14]

Depending on your scale-up, some 5P categories will be more relevant than others. Some may not be relevant at all.

I've worked with businesses scaling-up innovative technology for which an international patent program was the most critical constraint before launching overseas.

For other businesses, it can be the paperwork domain that causes the biggest headaches. One person I worked with, who was scaling-up a small HR analysis company, was being asked by his client whether he held the data on segregated servers in order to make sure that he kept their data separated from other clients' data. Everything he did was on one laptop! He had to answer 150-plus questions in a questionnaire on his IT security set-up because the questionnaire was part of the large corporation's procurement process, and they wouldn't give it up.

It can take time to work out all of the constraints specific to the market you are targeting. With the insurance claim repair business I led, it took longer to get the building licences across Australia than we thought it would. It took a lot more legwork in filing returns and giving details to the state building licence authorities. It was on our critical path and would have slowed us down a lot, had we not done the paperwork early enough.

---

13. ASIC: Australian Securities and Investment Commission. TGA: Therapeutic Goods Administration.
14. Corporate customers or channel partners may expect you to have a minimum quality of systems and processes, including the ISO standards for quality, data management, IT security, information security, health & safety, and other non-trivial requirements.

Fire Prevention, Not Firefighting

One of the biggest challenges in business is that often we reward people for the wrong things. Business leaders prize people who can deal with a crisis well — the firefighters — and don't spend so much time (or praise) on those who were thoughtful beforehand and made the crisis less likely — the fire prevention squad.

Sometimes you cannot anticipate a crisis — that is, when a constraint becomes a real showstopper for your business. But most times, looking at the issues through the 5P framework beforehand can help you avoid or at least minimise the impact of these constraints on your scale-up plan. The value of doing so can be large, and not just because your business may "dodge a bullet" by preventing an issue arising.

Any issue that needs urgent management will take mental attention from your people, who might otherwise be focused on building the business. It can, and it does, distract your leadership. The knock-on effect can be large, as scale-ups can "run off the road" if their management gets too distracted or over-stretched.

Even if it's not a crisis, there can be a large drain on your team if you have not considered the 5P constraints. For example, recent legislation on hot topics such as modern slavery and data integrity now require bigger companies to check that their supply chain (their suppliers) has excellent controls and policies related to these topics. Although it may seem irrelevant to you as a smaller business, you will find that the big businesses want to know that they're safe when dealing with you in these areas.

Two Points to Remember

Any scale-up will be an intense learning curve, even if you've done similar work before. "Not knowing what you don't know" is often one of the biggest constraints. You should:

- *base your assumptions on informed advice.* Check with regulators if it's a highly regulated industry, check with industry bodies, and look for general advice from people connected with the industry. Even a simple web search can sometimes yield surprising nuggets of detail.

- *bear in mind that this is only your first go*. You won't fully understand every constraint until you're underway. You will learn about new constraints all the time, but this first stage gives you a good baseline on areas to watch out for that might cause you major delays, increased costs, or other risks to your scale-up.

CHECKLIST: REVIEWING YOUR CONSTRAINTS

- **Use** the 5P framework as a **prompt** for the major constraints that you will need to consider as you move into the Scale stage of your scale-up.

- **Focus** on a maximum of 10 constraints — say, two per category. Don't worry if you have more in one category and none in another. Don't get sucked into a lot of detail at this stage, or you may find you "can't see the wood for the trees".

- **Check** the completeness of your list by looking at **external** perspectives. Look at competitor advertising and industry websites. Look at the industry bodies. Your competitors will also give you some idea of what's required.

- **Think** about your **internal** resources: Your team's capabilities, knowledge of regulations, and availability to complete compliance activities. These are the resources you've already got that will help you tackle the challenges you might run up against.

- **Test** your views based on **time:** How will the constraints change (or appear) based on the different stages of the S-curve? You should make sure you capture in your scale-up plan any major time-related constraint assumptions (e.g. "It will take this amount of time to get our licences, so we expect this is when we can start our business").

- **Test** your views based on **scale:** It may sound obvious, but systems scalability (and functionality) is usually critical to your success. I've been caught out by this when it's been left late in the build process. Don't rely on assumptions or assertions based on your pilot or small-scale volumes; do proper "performance and volume" (P&V) testing early on.

Now What?

Well done — you've just completed your Strategy Compass–Version 1.0! You now have a great summary of the pull and push factors that will affect your scale-up.

It also gives you a checklist for the capabilities that your business needs to deliver your scale-up strategy. Have you got the right resources, the right people, and the right focus in your business to achieve your goals? The Strategy Compass can help steer you to the right answers from the outset.

If you keep it up to date — as you strengthen your understanding, and as your scale-up moves from early stage to execution of your ramp-up — then you will also have an important tool to keep your team aiming at the most important elements for scale-up success.

You will always have more to do than you have time or resources. This is the norm in scale-ups. The trick is to always do the most important things first, even when they are difficult or unfamiliar. That's what the Strategy Compass will show you. *Go to the pain rather than avoid it*, says legendary fund manager and business guru Ray Dalio. Your Strategy Compass will show you not just the strengths of your strategy, but also the weaknesses. It will highlight the pain points you need to pay attention to, if you want to scale without fail.

Leveraging the Strategy Compass

Many people assume that a great business strategy will be obvious to execute. This process should have shown you that that assumption is not always correct!

The Strategy Compass gives you a tool to communicate your plans and assumptions to your nvestors, stakeholders and to your new staff as they come on board, because they won't all know the things you know.

In the next chapter, we'll build on your compass work and look at how you can construct your more detailed business plan as the basis for safely scaling at speed.

CHAPTER 4
Scale-Up with SOAP

In this chapter we'll take your Strategy Compass findings and convert them into a plan that you can deliver across 24 to 36 months. For this we will use an approach I call "strategy on a page", or SOAP, based on a simple template (with examples).

This approach will take your scale-up strategy into the Scale stage. It's an intermediate stage, but still important.

In my experience, it's hard to go from thinking about strategy to defining concrete actions. Our brains find it easier to think about strategy or detailed actions — but not both at the same time! So SOAP is a bridge to get you to clear targets you can aim your scale-up at, with specific actions to achieve those targets. SOAP also gives you more material to help you communicate the approach that you're taking across all of your stakeholders.

Old SOAP?

There is considerable value in summarising your key objectives. Nearly 20 years ago, Jim Collins (author of one of my favourite business books, *Good to Great*) popularised mobilising people around their employer's strategy — using what he called Big Hairy Audacious Goals, or BHAGs.

Further back, we can find the discipline of MBO, or Management by Objectives, first formalised by management guru Peter Drucker in his 1954 book, *The Practice of Management*. Drucker realised that many challenges in business performance came from people not knowing how they were going against their manager's expectations.

MBO makes those expectations explicit, in the form of agreed performance objectives.

It may seem strange to be talking about a performance-management system when you're only at the start of launching your scale-up. You will probably feel that you should focus your attention on the overall strategy, not on an MBO system. However, the point is to ensure you've expressed your high-level view in a framework that allows you to move your team smoothly from strategic objectives and onto the immediate next steps.

Making the SOAP

We build the SOAP template in stages, moving from strategic to tactical over three levels:

1. *Strategic Outcomes*: These are the tangible results being targeted. The "**What**" in numbers.
2. *Strategic Priorities*: The principal elements needed to deliver the outcomes, based on your Strategy Compass. These are the high level "**How**".
3. *Key Objectives:* The actions required to deliver the outcomes. Broken down into quarterly (or monthly) targets. This frames your scale-up outcomes over time — the "**When**".

The challenge is always to boil down a lot of thinking into a succinct summary. Summarising can be very hard. Various prominent writers echo the comment first made by French philosopher Blaise Pascal over 350 years ago in one of his letters, that "I have made this longer than usual because I have not had time to make it shorter". The time and effort it takes to put this summary together are worth it. Remember, this exercise **quantifies** your goal and makes it **tangible**, so you can make it easier to hit.

You might also feel reluctant to state your dreams or expectations in such concrete terms. Remember, this is the first pass of an iterative process. It will not be right on your first go, and you should not expect it to be. Consider it as the 80% solution that gets you a long way in the right direction. Without it, you will achieve much slower and less certain progress to your strategic goals.

The key thing from this exercise is not just to draft a tidy one-pager. Much of the value of building the SOAP comes from the assumptions that you will make, which lie behind your summary headlines. Write them down!

Over my career I learned valuable lessons from comparing initial assumptions with what actually happens. A written record allows you to be clear about what you need to fix, so you're not wondering, "What on earth were we thinking when we assumed that?". Where these assumptions are quantitative (e.g. sales conversion rates), they can be updated as your scale-up proceeds.

SOAP 1: Strategic Outcomes ("What")

The 5P Framework

The excellent news in building your SOAP, is that you will revisit the 5P framework that will be familiar to you from the prior chapter: profit & loss, people, process, property, paperwork.

To help you complete this work, I've provided a draft template (*see Figure 4.1, next page*). Because we are looking to quantify your goals, I suggest that you spread your expected outcomes out over the next three years. This will correspond roughly with the three different stages of the S-curve we talked about in Chapter 1: preparation (Start), growth (Scale), and maturity (Stabilise). If you think your timings are very different, then adjust the template headings as needed.

The important point here is to provide some idea of the **sequence** of the expected outcomes, and roughly **when** they will occur. This will help considerably when we move onto the detailed execution planning in the next chapter.

I found drafting the SOAP a very helpful exercise to clarify expectations for everyone involved. For example, the size of the ramp-up needed (such as, in numbers of staff) to get us from the pilot stage to full scale was easy to see so that everyone could understand the size of the challenge.

Strategic Outcomes

5P Focus Area	P&L		Performance		People			Place	Process
	$Rev	$EBITDA	KPI	Customer #	Sales	Dev team	Ops	Locations	Controls
YEAR 1	2M	0.2M	80%	100	2	5	4	NSW Metro	State licenses
YEAR 2	20M	2M	85%	5,000	4	10	8	National - NSW/VIC/ACT	ISO9001
YEAR 3	50M	5M	90%	20,000	8	12	12	International - NZ	Standard Operating Procedures

Strategic Priorities

Strategic Categories	Customers	Suppliers	Capabilities	Constraints
Major Objectives	B2B partner program	Contract main supplier	Build Dev team	State licenses
	Website fulfilment	Shipping systems	Hire leads	Onboarding controls
	Marketing program	Quality control process	Develop sales program	Data integrity - ISO 27001

Key Deliverables

Year	20x1			20x2			20x3		
	Q1	Q3	Q4	Q1	Q3	Q4	Q1	Q3	Q4
Recruit team	Hire 2 sales	2 Ops	Hire 5 dev	Hire 4 Ops			NZ head		
Secure supply contracts	Contract 1	Contract 2					Contract		
Build online channel	MVP website	V2		Online commerce	Roll out				Roll out
Develop B2B partner	Prospects ID		Sign contract	Develop			NZ prospect		
Source service partner	Procure		Contract		Expand			NZ service	
Complete licensing	Register		Complete					Renew	NZ license
Achieve ISO 9001	Start build	Audit		Registration					

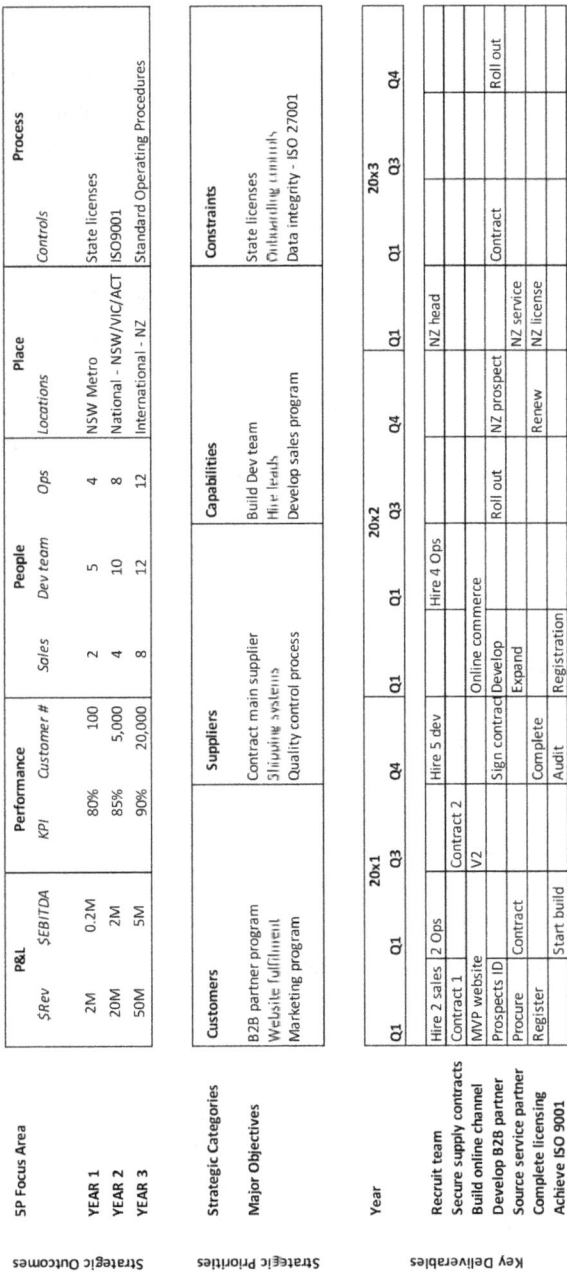

Figure 4.1: Strategy On A Page (SOAP) – Example

61

Shirt Sizing

Our first step in building the SOAP is to get a good idea of the probable size of the scale-up as it moves through its growth curve. We do this by completing an exercise I call "shirt sizing", based on a concept from the "agile" IT software development discipline. Just as you would buy a T-shirt based on a rough idea of your size (be it small, large, extra-large), so you estimate the size of your potential market (your "TAM", as we discussed in Chapter 2), and how much effort it takes to capture that opportunity.

The approach (in the agile world) emphasises speed over accuracy. For example, if you asked how long it would take to build an app or a system build, you would go through a shirt-sizing exercise. This removes the time taken to analyse development effort and instead uses the analogy of shirt sizes as a proxy for the amount of effort (and time) needed.

The agile IT method links "shirt sizes" to rough estimates of person-days of work. Large might be a hundred person-days' worth of development work. Extra small might be a day's worth. This estimation process allows the developers to assess how long it will take, and the resources required, when they don't have the time or the certainty to assess the business requirements in much detail beforehand.

For our purposes, we may not be as interested in person-day estimations as we are in how likely we are to convert market opportunities into real sales. The point here is to estimate the answers, even where there is little evidence, but recognise there will be different levels of certainty (which we can then test as we grow).

Another idea, borrowed from IT shirt sizing, is the practice of going through several rounds, to increase accuracy (from +/- 50% to closer to 90%) around the effort needed to deliver the required results.

You may feel that you don't need multiple rounds of estimation, as you have details developed already. For example, if you built an investor pitch deck, then you should have a solid idea of your addressable market, and therefore expected revenues from your business as it grows.

If you use the SOAP format, this will let you check whether your high-level strategic assumptions are well-grounded in reality. You can use

SOAP Strategic Outcomes as performance targets for the business: they focus management attention on risks and uncertainties in your plan, and the key things that you need to build or deliver to make the business results possible. You can record these in your Priorities and Deliverables sections, with more detail in your supporting record of key assumptions.

This exercise makes you work through your expected scale-up outcomes, breaking your "great idea" strategy into practical, how-I-am-going-to-do-it chunks.

CHECKLIST: SIZING YOUR STRATEGIC OUTCOMES

- **Summarise** the sales/revenue you expect over the next 3 years.
    - You should already have developed an idea of what your scale-up is aiming at from your prior strategic work (if not, you can use this exercise to do so, but allow more time and iterations to get to an answer you are happy with).
    - Check through your business model and **list the key assumptions** that drive volumes. I've included a template *(see Table 4.1)* with some key assumptions that you should be able to detail here.
    - If you get stuck on specific assumptions, **brainstorm** them with your team. Show the level of certainty in your answers.
    - List any **assumptions** that you think will significantly affect revenues, including those with the least certainty. You might be uncertain about future conversion rates (e.g. sales calls made to sales achieved).
- Based on your expected revenue profile over three years, estimate the likely outcomes in terms of **people** (how many, what functions), **process** (quality rates, volumes), **property** (include patents or other IP if this is important), and **paperwork** (e.g. regulatory or customer formal requirements). Flip back and review Chapter 3's comments on the 5Ps, which may help you complete this section.

- From these outcomes, consider your likely **P&L** (based on revenues less costs arising from the other 4Ps).

- Ensure your answers on the SOAP are **summary only**. Put further information, assumptions and explanations into your supporting documents. You can use the SOAP milestones for communication and execution planning for your scale-up, so this is not the place for extensive detail, but for succinct headlines.

Table 4.1: Shirt Sizing your Scale-up Opportunity — Some Assumptions

Suggested Approach

- Focus on key assumptions that drive volumes (revenue and operational activity).

- Aim to quantify outcomes to support resource planning (capabilities, people required), sales & marketing planning, and financial scoping.

- Use bucket sizing for impact or value if you can't confirm numbers, e.g. XL/L/M/S/XS.

- Assess the sensitivity of your assumptions: focus on those with the biggest impact on your success, or level of effort required.

- Assess the certainty of your assumption: this highlights further research is needed.

- Complete two rounds: initial estimation at high level, and then re-run with more detail.

- You may find it helpful to review quarterly to increase the accuracy of your strategy and your operating model.

Note: modify the example questions as required for your specific business.

Example Assumptions	Test	Answer *or* XL/L/M/S/XS	Certainty (H-M-L)
Size of market opportunity — total revenues available	Is this addressable? (Can *you* really compete for this?)		
Margin expected – %	What do competitors achieve in the market now?		
Share of market achievable – Year 1, 2, 3	How long to gain customers?		
Number of customers	How many customers to achieve revenues? Are they all similar value, buying power?		
Volume of product/average value cf service	How much quantity (products sold, services subscribed etc.) is needed to achieve targets?		
Product/service — key features	Time, quality, reliability, trust, price, simplicity, ease of use — what is the differentiator?		
Example Capabilities	Sample questions		
Sales volume — which channels are most valuable?	How many salespeople needed? How to achieve leads (how much advertising)/ conversion rate?		
Delivery/service model	How many people to deliver product or service?		
Infrastructure model to deliver and service	Equipment for staff, channels, premises?		
Software and IT systems	Apps, websites for sales & service? (Note: internal systems = part of more detailed plans.)		
Legal & IP constraints	Are there any major licensing, legal hurdles or IP (e.g. patent) steps needed to complete? How long/ how much effort will they take? (XL -> XS)		

Which Version?

As you step through the next section of SOAP (on your Priorities), you may want to revisit your initial Strategic Outcomes. This is normal, and where the SOAP process adds value. You will be cross-checking your assumptions against each part of your business model and vice versa.

This cross-checking ensures consistency in your planning and avoids the sudden discovery of a planning "black hole" as you proceed. For example, it would be unwelcome news if you ended up with a growth plan that requires you to hire more people in one week than you are able to onboard in one month.

As you edit and adjust your assumptions and outcomes, my strong advice is to implement **version control** on these different versions. Not only for your SOAP, but for all your documents. By this I mean giving them a unique reference or file name every time you make a change. It may seem pedantic, but I have seen the value of this when making adjustments to extensive sets of documents over many months. You end up with dozens of versions that, without good control, will confuse everyone and make it impossible to track errors and omissions.

Don't put off this important habit. Number your papers and make each change a unique version. *Version control is essential.*

Accuracy v Uncertainty

The novelty of a scale-up makes it more likely that your future business model may not be clear in every detail. But if you cannot answer many of the key questions with certainty after several iterations, then you should consider whether you need to run a short (3–6 months) pilot to test your assumptions and processes.

It's possible that a pilot of the new business model has shown that your scale-up needs to change approach ("pivot") to address a bigger market opportunity. Here, your SOAP is likely to be more speculative, and will be harder to complete. But the template can help to test the alternative business model, which you will refine as you develop your new business approach. This may be very relevant in a tech business that needs to adjust its approach to "cross the chasm" from early adopters to the mass market, as we discussed in Chapter 2.

In completing the strategic outcomes of the SOAP template, your aim is to generate specific goals from a sea of uncertainty. It is a "work in progress" that will change. I have seen finance teams take these summaries and use them as the basis for committed budgets and annual P&L forecasts. Don't let that happen! These are not financial forecasts; they are planning tools to ensure you align your scale-up resources properly against your most important goals.

SOAP 2: Strategic Priorities ("How")

Now that you have put down your expected strategic outcomes in the 5P domains, you can focus on the "how" — the key elements that will get you to your outcomes. The splendid news is that this section also draws on work you have already completed in the Strategy Compass, and in the assumptions you have logged when you considered your strategic outcomes in the section above.

Strategic Priority Domains

Three of the sections relate to the Strategy Compass domains: **Customers, Suppliers, Constraints**. You should add any **Competitor**-focused points into your Constraints section, as these are not usually the major focus for a scale-up. The fourth section captures any major internal **Capabilities** you may need to build to deliver the scale-up.

This stage of the SOAP ensures that you have expressed the strategic goals of the business in terms of **specific management priorities**. Your team can use this summary to confirm their focus on the most important things and identify any gaps or issues that need fixing. If you have investors or external advisors, this also usefully keeps in front of them a summary of management's key priorities and makes it easier for them to see the big picture.

Eisenhower and the Importance of Focus

In any business, often the hardest thing is to keep everyone (yourself included) focused on doing the things that matter. It's a particular challenge in scale-ups, where enthusiasm is high and experience of what does (or does not) work is low. Yet we see the benefit of tight focus in execution in many places. Martial arts, for example, teach that the application of focus overcomes brute strength in combat. In his book *Good to Great*, Jim Collins says, "Most of what we are doing in business is a waste of energy. If we ignore it or stop doing it, our lives will be simpler, and our results will have actually improved."

This section will be the basis on which you will later build programs of work. You need to keep the list short, and to the point.

It's easy to say this but very hard to do, whatever size of business you are running. In fact, it's hard to remain focused on the important things when there may be more pressing matters demanding your attention.

The need to balance important issues with urgent ones was something that perplexed Dwight D Eisenhower, the 34th President of the USA, who in the 1950s had complex issues like ending the Korean War, coping with the start of the Cold War, and building the USA's now-famous Interstate Highway System on his plate. A successful military leader in World War II, it's perhaps no surprise that he considered that "In preparing for battle I have always found that plans are useless, but planning is indispensable."

Stephen Covey's book *The Seven Habits of Highly Effective People* quotes Eisenhower as using a 2x2 tool to help him decide how to prioritise his many competing priorities. We now know this as the **Eisenhower Decision Matrix**. You can see an example at *Figure 4.2*.

This highlights that it is easy for us to pay attention to the tasks that are both important and urgent — the first quadrant in the matrix. But it is in the DECIDE Quadrant — tasks that are important but <u>not</u> urgent — which can be hard to do unless you keep them in full view. Management attention should focus firmly on these elements.

To ensure you have assessed your strategic priorities correctly, put your current activity plans into the Eisenhower Matrix to see where they sit. This exercise will help you keep these *important but not urgent* tasks in front of you and your team, not pushed to the bottom of to-do lists and forgotten.

Is It Strategic or Tactical?

I have seen some leadership teams get bogged down in trying to work out whether their "to do" list was sufficiently strategic, or too tactical. Namely: what is appropriate to log here, rather than in a more detailed activity plan later on?

My advice is not to get over-focused on definitions. The Eisenhower Matrix can help you distinguish between urgent (mostly tactical) and important (mostly strategic). However, if something is a complete showstopper — such as you don't have a developer to build a key part of your system — then I would put it in here, perhaps as part of a broader point (e.g. "build development team").

For me, the key test is whether we will do these points in one quarter (3 months). If the answer is mostly yes, then I would say they are probably too tactical (i.e. "do t now"), and we should look further ahead, to what you need in 6–12 months as you grow.

You may find it easiest to revisit this point once you've gone through the last stage of the SOAP, putting in more detailed objectives against a timeline. This will help you see whether you have got the level right in setting your strategic priorities.

	URGENT	NOT URGENT
IMPORTANT	**DO** *Important AND Urgent* *(Immediate opportunities* *Major problems* *People leadership)*	**DECIDE** *Important, NOT Urgent* *(Time with friends, family* *Longer term planning* *Exercise)*
NOT IMPORTANT	**DELEGATE** *NOT Important, BUT Urgent* *(Answering certain queries* *Booking travel* *Approving actions)*	**DELETE** *NOT Important, NOT Urgent* *(Time wasters* *Junk mail* *Trivia)*

Figure 4.2: The Eisenhower Decision Matrix

SOAP 3: Key Deliverables

Early in my career, I got a project job designing additional features into a banking product. I was a minor part of a much larger program, which was rebuilding the way this major UK bank processed payments. Every day, millions of payments worth many billions in value went through their systems, so it was a significant program with lots of management attention. One thing I used to hate was that every week, the project control manager would come round and ask me how I had done on my tasks the previous week, and what my expected progress would be the next week. Then he would publish that as part of the wider program project management progress report, so that senior management

CHECKLIST: DOCUMENTING YOUR STRATEGIC OUTCOMES

- Review your 4 Strategy Compass domains and look at the points you captured there. You should transfer across into the SOAP your most important elements for success/ biggest capability gaps.

- If not sure about the top priorities, brainstorm with your team and rank them.

- Use the Eisenhower Matrix to ensure you haven't overlooked the Decide Quadrant items.

- You should limit your priorities to 3–5 maximum per domain. I would normally expect to see 3 priorities per domain as a healthy number.

- Focus on the priorities or key capabilities to get you to scale (i.e. through the first 2 stages of the S-curve). Don't forget, you'll be reviewing these as you go, and the things you need to think about when you are at scale will become clearer as you get into stage 2 (Scale).

- I suggest you review these capabilities every quarter, to check on progress and relevance.

- You will look to build metrics to track progress in a later stage. You should use these priorities as the start point for setting KPIs (key performance objectives) for the team.

could see clearly whether or not we were on track. There was no escaping the spotlight if your bit of the program wasn't going to plan!

This was my introduction to large-scale project management. It was a painful grind at times, but very necessary to ensure that so many diverse parts of the program remained aligned. Detailed follow-up like this ensured that the program delivered all of its objectives within the expected deadlines.

Linking Strategic Priorities to Specific Projects

The good news is that project-management tools and practices have developed over the years, so now we have useful tools like Microsoft Project and Trello, which help track what we're doing with ease. If you're building a business fast, you will need to use something like this, or at least some of the work scheduling and resource-planning disciplines that underpin them.

Often it's hard to link the detail of the project work explicitly to the higher-level business objectives. If you've ever had to explain your MS Project plan to an interested but uninvolved stakeholder, you will be familiar with that glazed look that comes over their faces after a few minutes of talking them through dependencies and assumptions. Not fun for either of you!

This is where this last stage of SOAP comes in. It doesn't replace the need to do that bottom-up project planning, but it provides a clear link between what your team is doing, and what will happen. It provides an easy-to-see record of those milestones and makes it easy to see how they support the strategic priorities you have laid out. You will find this makes it a useful tool to communicate what your planned milestones are across the business, with as few glazed eyes as possible.

Approach

This last stage of SOAP captures the major milestones and actions required to deliver the scale-up outcomes and puts them into a clear timeframe.

- **Make your milestones quarterly** (i.e. Q1, Q2 of the year), spread across the planned timeline for your scale-up. You'll see from the example that it translates the strategic priorities (on the left-hand column) into deliverables across the page that are more specific and detailed.

- **Don't be surprised if you can't easily get it on one page**. The level of detail you might need even at this high level could require multiple pages. By all means build these — but then summarise so only the most important are on your "top level" SOAP document. This is the document you will use to communicate to staff and stakeholders on priorities and progress, so it needs to be simple enough that they can digest it easily.
- **Maintain your milestones and supporting assumptions under change control**. Update them monthly. Take each strategic priority and look at what you need to do to achieve it. You should also maintain version control over your assumptions and link them to your deliverables. As you learn more, you will find it easier to track the impact of any changes into your planned outcomes this way, and it will make it easy for everyone to know why and when you've changed your milestones.
- **Double-check your dependencies**. Make sure you have re-confirmed the availability of whatever you need (from the 5Ps) that is essential for your scale-up. Highlight critical dependencies or constraints and track them closely in your execution plans.
- **Add some buffer time** — *make the milestone earlier than you absolutely have to do it*. That way if you slip your deadline for any excellent reason, you will not endanger the scale-up by late delivery.

Remember the 80/20 Rule

Remember, this is an iterative process. No plan will be perfect: the trick is to capture the key elements that allow you to proceed quickly and safely onto the next step of your scale-up. The financial plan (budget) and the more detailed plan you will build next to execute this strategy will inevitably cause changes to your timings. Until you've done some more validation, expect these details to change. I used to put "Draft" or some other obvious caveat on my first versions, so that stakeholders would know to expect major changes.

Another 80/20 I've observed is the number of milestones identified for the first 12 months, compared to years 1, 2 and 3 of your scale-up plan. It's always easier to see what you need to do in the near term rather than further out in time. This "front-loading" of deliverables in this section seems natural and you shouldn't worry if you find it hard to list what you will do in 18, 24, and 36 months. However, it is worth testing your team on whether this means there is not enough DECIDE Quadrant thinking going into these milestones. Provided you do this, and also a monthly or quarterly review, it will be easy to identify the deliverables, and then add these to your SOAP as time passes and your scale-up progresses.

As you revise your milestones, you may find it useful to colour-code newly identified or amended deliverables. Your aim is always to learn from the changes you have had to make in your original plan.

Conclusion

I thought about calling this section the "Wash Up", but you've probably heard enough soap-based allusions!

Now that you've worked through this section, you will have completed your first outline scale-up plan. Well done! If you have done this by translating your existing plans into the SOAP format, then I expect and hope this will have highlighted several points for you and your team to tighten up or clarify.

I've found that to complete the Key Deliverables section and make the milestones realistic, a basic project management mindset and some skills are essential. It can be harder than people think to define and plan how long it will take to deliver specific outcomes. This is an area where external advice, practical experience or even some project management support may save you some grief (and a lot of re-planning) later on.

What's Next

In the next chapter, we'll take the SOAP conclusions into the next stage, building the business case and execution plan that ensures your scale-up can deliver within its financial resources and capabilities.

CHAPTER 5

ScaleCast: Escape from the "Valley of Death"

There are many milestones to celebrate as you build your business: your first product launch, your first customers, your first investors. These are all great moments. But the most exciting moment must be when your business "gets to cash"— that is, break-even. This means you have climbed out of the "Valley of Death", that period of negative cash flow almost every scale-up goes through, where costs exceed income. It's a scary place to be, and *some businesses never escape it.* That's why it's called the Valley of Death.

Recent research[15] from the digital agency Fractl on 193 scale-up failures in the USA, showed that **more than half** of the companies had a business model that would not work, or they just ran out of money. This tells us that these businesses either hadn't fully tested their key assumptions or they hadn't done enough planning around the financial aspects of their business.

In this chapter I'm going to look at what you need to do to make it safely through the inevitable financial stresses. It's based on doing well what many business leaders find boring or difficult: the financial plan.

---

15. *Decoding Startup Failure: Why 193 Failed Startups Didn't Survive* https://www.frac.tl/work/marketing-research/why-startups-fail-study/

Are You in Financial Denial?

The financial aspects of running a business seem to separate the world into three kinds of people:

- Spreadsheet **Builders** — otherwise known as analysts and finance folk
- Spreadsheet **Avoiders** — unfortunately, most entrepreneurs, most of the time
- Spreadsheet **Savants** (or Savvy) — financially wise business leaders

Some scale-up business leaders have surprised me with how little reference they make to spreadsheet plans in general. Often these are created only to satisfy investors, or confirm a specific decision, already made in principle. Yet, done well, a spreadsheet forecast can be one of the most useful tools available to a scale-up leader. It can be used to detail plans, test alternative scenarios, and model the impact of events as the scale-up proceeds. It's also a powerful way to identify the key drivers of value to your team, and to highlight specific performance targets.

Now you may be thinking: hang on, I've got a finance person for all this stuff. Or, even better. I've built the business case and got funding, so there are other smart people who have looked at this and put their money in, so it's got to be good, right?

Maybe not. Let's consider three important points:

1. ***"Finance" means many different things***. All of which are important to your scale-up, and all needing different kinds of financial expertise. It's unlikely one person will be able to cover everything, nor would it be a good idea. The skills and focus needed to build your financial model, raise capital, and manage the day-to-day financials are quite different. A good Finance director understands each function, but should look for specific expertise to deliver the best results.

2. *Investors don't always get it right.* Case studies from the original first dot.com boom and bust (1998–2000) show that even smart backers put large amounts of money into ventures that with hindsight were never going to make it out of the valley of death. Take a look at Boo.com, Webvan, and Pets.com (*see Table 5.1*).

Table 5.1: Three Dotcom Financial Management Disasters

Boo.com (1998–2000)

Boo.com was an online consumer fashion web store, founded by Ernst Malmsten and ex-model Kajsa Leander in 1998, which closed in mid-2000 having spent over £150M. At its peak the business had achieved only 300,000 customers and £100,000 in turnover per month.

It was famous for a clunky, media-heavy website (complete with trendy avatar, Ms Boo) that didn't work well in the low-bandwidth world of the 1990s where most customers were using dial-up modems.

Costs ran out of control, with more than 400 overpaid staff and a jet-set expenses-funded lifestyle for its leaders, which made no sense given the scale and stage of the business. When the dotcom bust hit with the business needing millions every month to pay its basic running costs, its backers and bankers walked away.

Webvan (1999–2001)

Webvan was a US-based business that delivered groceries such as bread and vegetables it sold online through its website. Within 2 years it spent over US$1Billion, hiring 4,000 employees and expanding nationally, building a chain of advanced purpose-built warehouses and an enormous dedicated fleet of vans and lorries delivering products into multiple large US cities

---

During its short life Webvan went public; it was valued at one point at over US$1.2Billion. It then bought a major competitor, HomeGrocer, but by 2001 declared bankruptcy and closure after losing $127M in the first quarter of that year alone. Although the idea of home grocery shopping was not bad, the inexperienced management team at Webvan decided to take on the might of America's supermarket giants like Walmart, building their company from scratch with no financial or strategic advantage.

Pets.com (1998–2000)

Pets.com sold pet food and accessories in 2000, and like Webvan spent hundreds of millions of dollars on infrastructure, marketing and warehousing. It aimed to grow quickly on the basis that it would make a profit before its seed money ran out. But the only way it could attract shoppers was to sell below cost, spending $46 on advertising for every $10 in sales during 1999.

The company was eventually sold to a rival at a knock-down price in November 2000, after realising it would take at least 5 years to earn the $300M per year it needed simply to break-even.

Common Themes: These businesses failed in an earlier period where online access was slow, and most consumers were not comfortable giving their credit card details online to third-part vendors. We live in different circumstances today, but these businesses are great examples of failing to pay attention to the basics of testing their business models and building robust financial forecasts to demonstrate the viability of their execution plans.

Table 5.2. Dick Smith — Wrecked by Rebates

Dick Smith was an iconic Australian high-street electronics retailer founded in 1968 and run by its eponymous owner until the 20-store chain (and mail-order catalogue business) was sold to Woolworths in 1980–82. In 2012 it was bought by a private equity business, floated on the ASX in 2013 for A$520M, and then appeared to trade successfully for several years with sales over $1.5Billion per annum and over 360 stores in Australia and New Zealand.

After the share price collapsed in early January 2016, the company went quickly into administration. The stores closed and the Dick Smith brand-name was sold to online rival kogan.com. The last physical Dick Smith store closed in May 2016, with creditors left holding losses of more than $260M.

The speed of the collapse highlights Dick Smith's poor underlying profitability. This was the result of a business model that appears to have focused on short-term profits rather than sustainable business. Dick Smith took rebates from suppliers for products that then sold slowly or not at all. The company booked the rebates as revenue, but the products then failed to sell, and often had to be written off as obsolete stock. Rebates were doubly attractive to Dick Smith because they were booked as profits in the month that the stock was purchased, not when it was sold, which effectively accelerated the business' apparent revenue growth

While rebates were not the only problem with Dick Smith's performance or strategy, they highlight how the business had become focused on dressing-up its financials, at the expense of stocking and selling products that customers wanted. Rebates from suppliers distorted the financial health of the business, over-inflating profits in the short-term but understating true costs of this support from its suppliers..

3. ***Paper profits won't save a failing business, however big it is.*** The collapse of major high-street name Dick Smith in 2018 (*see Table 5.2*) came about after declaring record profits. But revenues had been inflated by including rebates from suppliers to take less popular stock, which could not be sold and eventually had to be written off for tens of millions of dollars.

The common theme here is that the *financial success of the business depends on its business leader* (not its head of finance). Although finance teams (and spreadsheet "builders") can run the processes that ensure your numbers are going in the right direction, it's the leaders of the business that make the assumptions and take the decisions that lead to eventual success or failure.

Introducing the ScaleCast

Whatever your comfort level with financials, your business will benefit from a robust financial plan to avoid spending too much time in the "Valley of Death". This is more than budget or cash flow, or even business projection (although it should be aligned with all of these).

What you need is a **living forecast model** of how your business will perform as it scales up, with operational drivers delivering financial outcomes that you will be tracking on a monthly (or even weekly) basis. By "living", I mean something that is adaptable and used to make business decisions (e.g. identifying when you need to hire more staff), and against which you track performance. As you discover your outcomes are different from your original assumptions (as they will be), then you can update your plan to capture these new learnings.

I call this living scale-up model the "ScaleCast", upon which you will be able to build your business, and from which your finance team can also confirm your financial budget and cash-flow projections.

Done well, the ScaleCast will give you the step-by-step framework to get to break-even and beyond. In the large Sydney-based scale-up that I led in 2018, it was a critical tool to validate our business case assumptions and get us out of pilot and into national roll-out. Without it, we would have soon lost sight of our weekly progress and hit an enormous cliff.

Our ScaleCast showed us that at one point we would need to hire more people in one month than we had in the entire business until then! We re-worked our plans, smoothed out our lumpy growth, and adjusted our model assumptions based on our real-life experience. As a result we got to national scale in 18 months: record pace in the eyes of the stakeholders.

So building a ScaleCast can make an enormous difference to the scale and pace of your execution. It can show you the *scale* of resources required and *when* you will need them to deliver your scale-up. It highlights the key assumptions or decisions that you need to test and refine, and also shows when the scale-up will become cash positive, with the level of funding (the depth of the "valley") needed to get there. The value of this can be seen when you compare different breakeven timings (*see Figure 5.1*).

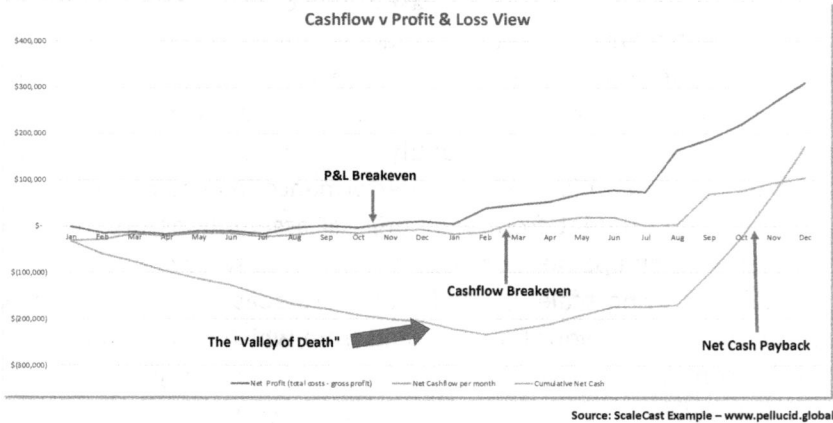

Source: ScaleCast Example – www.pellucid.global

Figure 5.1: Different Views on Break-Even

Where Are You Starting From?

It's highly likely you already have a budget and financial plan. In which case you will find the following comments helpful as a check on your approach, even if you decide not to build a complete ScaleCast to supplement your existing tools.

Alternatively, you may not have detailed your financial plans yet. If you are starting from scratch, you may find it useful to look at the appendix first, as this goes through some of the basics to consider in building a financial forecast model. There are numerous online tutorials on how to build basic financial models, some of which I have linked to my website, www.pellucid.global.

The ScaleCast Approach

Successful businesses need to earn more money than they spend over time, to survive and make a profit. These key concepts can be captured through looking at your business plans laid out over a ScaleCast. This should run for at least two years, but preferably three.

Your ScaleCast should be built in 5 steps, which I will go through one by one in this chapter.

1. Based on the work you've done for the Strategy Compass, consider the **income** side of the plan: your *customers* and the *revenue* you expect to achieve from them

2. Then add the **BAU costs** to deliver the services that those customers buy.

3. Third, consider the non-BAU or **change-related costs** to deliver the scale-up: what's needed to manage the growth during the scale-up period. We'll look at why this distinction is important.

4. Next, review the **impact of time** on working capital, and how the business and the dollars change during the scale up.

5. Finally, consider some "**Do's and Don'ts**" to avoid painful mistakes when you put your ScaleCast together, summarised in the *Checklist: Test Your ScaleCast Thinking.*

In this chapter we will cover the key call-outs in each of these sections, with further detail provided in the appendix if you need to get into more detail on *how* to build the ScaleCast. To keep this simple, I will use a general example ScaleCast created to illustrate the main points. You can find an electronic version of this template at my website, www.pellucid.global.

Income: Customers and Revenue

This section defines business customer growth and expected returns on these customers, based on your understanding of the market. You will need to break down these assumptions into specific monthly targets.

Let's be clear: If you don't have good detail on your true north (your customers), *the rest of your ScaleCast is likely to be wrong or irrelevant.*

You may have heard of the garbage in, garbage out (GIGO) principle. If you put wrong things into your process, a system, or your software, it's likely that what comes out will be wrong. The Fractl study I quoted earlier pinpoints *insufficient market demand* as a major fail reason for businesses not scaling.

Think of the customer as your investor: if you can't show them enough value to make them want to buy, compared to the "do nothing" or "do something else" option, then why would they buy from you?

The good news is that you will be able to use the work you did for the Strategy Compass exercise in Chapter 3. What you can do now is use the ScaleCast to test your key assumptions. For example:

- *Expected gross margin*: How much you will make once you consider the cost of customer acquisition and sales. This gives you a very good yardstick to measure whether the business is making enough money from the market.
- *Detailed weekly forecasts:* These describe how you get to your scale targets and will highlight any implausible steps. For example, expecting enormous growth over quiet periods, or month to month huge changes in volumes, which then require you to hire and train a lot of new people.

- *The relationship between pricing/customer acquisition and costs:* The cost of acquiring customers (and keeping them, through service management) can drive longer-term costs. Make sure your assumptions are consistent with both your revenues and your costs.

Making Assumptions in an Unknown Market

This is an area where some assumptions may be unknown when you start. If that's the case, you need to look for reference points in the market or make informed guesses to fill in any blanks.

You might think, "It's innovation, we can't be accurate around customer uptake. It's all new". That's true but remember that this is a tool to learn from. It only works if you put in your best estimates. We're not expecting this to be 100% right, especially at the outset. *Perfection is the enemy of progress,* said Winston Churchill. That's why it's better to concentrate on making informed guesses and adjusting your ScaleCast numbers when you have better data from actual experience.

Because of this uncertainty, it's a good idea to check your revenue assumptions for possible sensitivity to changes — what's known as *stress testing.* If your revenues were 10% lower than expected, or took three months longer to come through, how would that affect your bottom line?

CHECKLIST: BUILDING THE INCOME SCALECAST

- **Establish your key assumptions.** These should be your key drivers of growth — for example, customer numbers, and value in dollar terms per customer. If individual channels are a big part of the delivery model, such as online and social media, then you should also define your expected usage of them

---

- **Lay out your expected growth over time:** You've already defined that in your SOAP, in the year 1–3 timeline. Now you need to break this down into monthly totals. It's reasonable to assume a period of slower take-off, then faster growth during your scale-up timeline.

- **Plot out the monthly sales and customer volumes in terms of quantities and dollar value:** Allow for slack periods, such as Easter, Christmas, and summer holidays, if these are likely to affect your sales. Make it realistic, including likely fluctuations and seasonal variations.

- **Express goals in operational units not just financial:** Usually businesses express their goals as dollar targets. But if you only detail your plans in dollars, then you will miss some important details. Operational **volumes** (e.g. service calls, orders, shipments) are relevant because they are the elements that drive your costs. They're essential for capacity and service planning from the operational side, which we'll cover in the Costs section.

Costs: BAU

If your business has completed its start-up phase, or you're an established business now looking to grow fast, I expect you will already have a budget. If not, I recommend that you leverage help from your accountant, or accounting software such as Xero or MYOB, which can provide the basic cost categories you need to consider.

Your financial budget should be separate and additional to your ScaleCast. The budget and ScaleCast assumptions should align on the bottom line, but the ScaleCast focuses on what drives change on a monthly basis, not the statutory financial view.

As a crude example: if you're underwater for three months and above water for nine months, then you're on average above water — provided you don't drown sometime during those first three months!

Your focus on costs in the ScaleCast is to confirm how your business case assumptions play out over time. There are some important learning points from getting into *just enough detail* on these operational drivers of cost. It's the 80/20 Rule again.

Doesn't Finance Have This Covered?

You might think this is just a technical finance thing like a budget, and not very important at this stage. But it's not a budget; it's a key part of validating your business case and your scale-up approach.

The viability of the business depends on being able to get the business to profit. This depends on the actual costs of the business being justified by the revenues that you can extract (which you worked out in the first section above). You want to avoid the fate of those scale-up businesses I mentioned earlier, which failed from having a non-viable business model, or running out of money.

Non-viable Business Model: I worked with a start-up a few years ago that offered software to other SMEs. It needed to distribute its services to small businesses based in each local government area, not just at state level within Australia. We worked out that our distribution costs were huge, once we saw that we needed a lot more on-the-ground local capability to make the sale happen. The true cost of acquiring and servicing those customers made it unviable, so the business didn't go ahead. Disappointing, but better to have worked it out before burning money and goodwill doing something that would not be profitable, even at scale.

Running out of Cash: The second major kind of issue you want to avoid is what bankers call "over-trading". This is where a good idea needs more working capital than you have in the business. This is easier to fix than the first problem, but your business also needs to understand and avoid it. Otherwise you could run out of money, even while you are making profitable sales.

My first exposure to this issue came many years ago, when I was banker to a business that was importing high-quality bricks and roof-tiles into the UK from Europe. They were getting lots of new business, but their costs were coming in before their sales revenues were. Although they were doing lots of business, their cash flow was steadily shrinking. They needed more working capital to support bigger sales, and they hadn't worked that out.

I spoke with the lead director, and he asked, "What's a cash flow?" That wasn't a good sign for a lending banker! With a better handle on their working capital needs (and more capital), they might have been a successful business, but with neither of these things they had to rein in their growth, or risk running out of money and going bust.

ScaleCast Approach to BAU Costs

The level of detail needed in your ScaleCast cost model depends on the complexity of your business. You want to confirm your **operational capacity** to service your customers, not just **financial** capacity.

I have seen scale-up businesses with very complex sales and service needs. This complexity makes it hard to work out the **size** of operational capacity required, **when** that capacity is needed, and **how much** it costs. Log your assumptions and build them into an explicit plan — your ScaleCast. Otherwise it will be difficult to understand the pace of growth needed in your infrastructure, such as how many skilled staff you might need to hire, and when.

CHECKLIST: SCALECAST PRINCIPLES FOR YOUR COST MODEL

- **Distinguish between running costs and growth costs**: Mixing these two means you will not easily see your "normal" operating costs or be able to confirm your profitability.

- **Separate fixed costs from variable costs:** Being clear about which costs increase with scale, and those that don't, will help you confirm the dynamics of your scale-up business case. If your costs are mostly fixed (e.g. writing and publishing a book), then every extra sale past break-even is profit: your business is geared to scale (a good thing). Large software companies such as Microsoft (MSFT) are good examples of this. MSFT is a 45-year-old business these days. It's growing sales well (+53% over the last 5 years, to $143 billion in the year to June 2020), with net profit margins consistently around the 30% mark. *This is about three times the average of other profitable businesses.*

- **Focus most on getting right the high-impact assumptions**: These are the factors that will have the biggest impact on your ScaleCast numbers. For example, if your service teams take 4 days to close off a customer request rather than 2 days, that may seem unimportant when volumes are low. But this represents a *halving* of their expected capacity! When you have dozens or hundreds of operators, the cost difference (and increased staff needed) from this small assumption change will have a <u>massive</u> impact on your scale-up plan. In the models I have built, key assumptions are identified as inputs that can be reviewed and changed based on practical experience as the business grows (*see Figure 5.2*).

- **Iterate your ScaleCast model as you progress:** Review your initial operational assumptions and cost drivers, and update from experience. This should be done monthly, but

I suggest you update your model whenever you gain new information that brings major change to your assumptions.

- **Review contingency:** It's normal in a business to budget extra to allow for unforeseen events. This can be 10% in most projects, but in an uncertain environment you might want to go to 20% or even more. The point is not to *forecast* this spend, but to ensure you have *budgeted* for the potential need for it.

- **Confirm your strategic costs are included:** Based on the Strategy Compass elements you've identified through SOAP, ensure you have included these costs. If you're planning for international expansion, for example, don't ignore the cost of this strategic development.

- **Double-check you have included the costs of management:** As you grow you will need larger management teams to manage the larger business. If you are a people-based service, for example, you will need more team leaders. Software businesses may need more product; business and technology development specialist leaders, who in turn will need managing.

- **Don't account for efficiency gains from scale until later:** Scale brings benefits by giving you more revenue to apply against your fixed costs. However, this increased operational efficiency requires increased management attention, to sustain the value or quality of what you're delivering to your customers when you have more volume. Over time, most businesses should see economies of scale where increased efficiency will reduce your total operational costs. But simultaneously scaling-up and increasing efficiency would require an exceptional management team! My suggestion is that your ScaleCast plans *assume operational efficiency gains only after your scale-up period.*

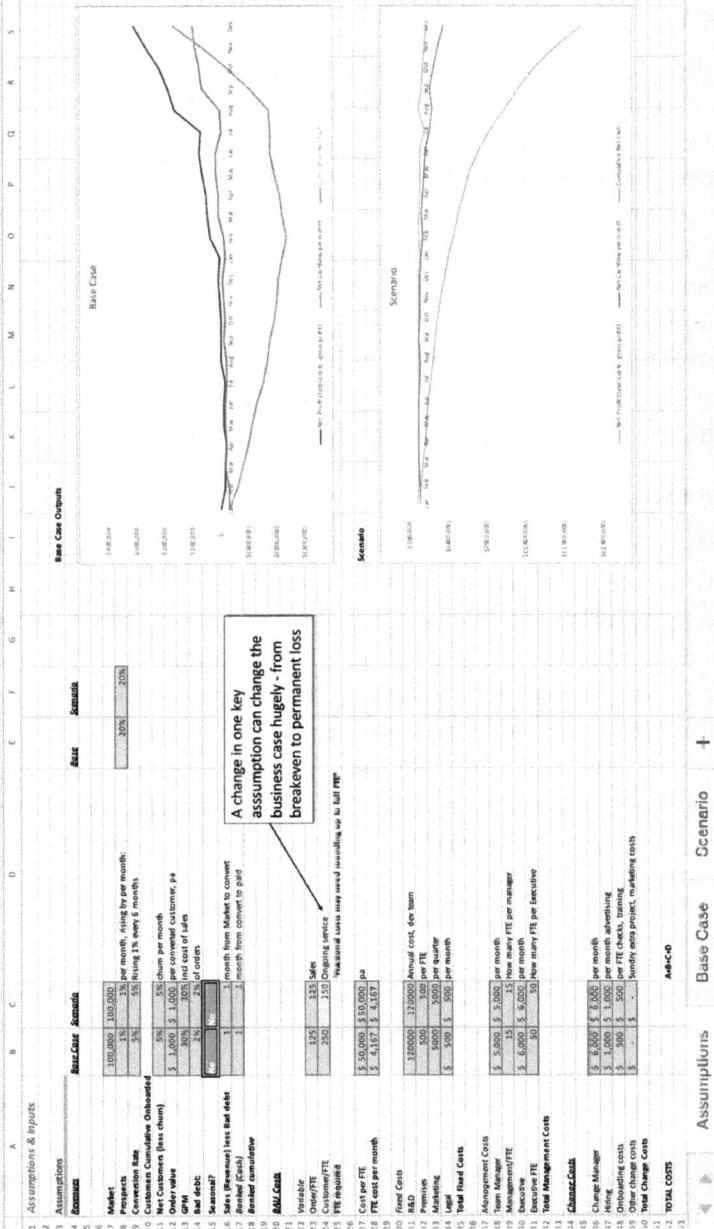

A change in one key
assumption can change the
business case hugely - from
breakeven to permanent loss

Figure 5.2: Input Assumptions

Summary

If you have categorised your costs properly, then by completing these two sections you will have your "BAU ScaleCast": revenues less operating costs. Like a good financial cash flow, this will show you your break-even point — where during the scale-up your rising revenues surpass your fixed costs.

The ScaleCast also ties these financial outcomes back to specific operational assumptions. If the bottom line does not match your projections (and it rarely does), then you will understand why not. You can then **fix your assumptions** so that the scale-up forecast is more accurate. Or you can **fix your operating performance**, as the ScaleCast will highlight which elements are not performing as expected.

Change (Scale-Up) Costs

Now that you have detailed the "run the business" or RTB costs, your ScaleCast needs to consider another important category of costs in order to be accurate. This will include the costs of any other elements you need to manage the growth of your business during its rapid scale-up period: **the costs of "changing the business" (CTB)**.

These CTB costs can represent temporary increases to **existing** categories of RTB costs but will also include **new cost** categories. Examples might be the costs of hiring specific "change management" expertise; or new kinds of marketing spend to boost revenue growth, such as a product launch event.

Why Bother?

If you keep RTB and CTB costs in separate buckets, you will find it easier to keep senior management and investors comfortable with the progress of your plans.

A few years ago I sat in an executive management meeting explaining a large proposed scale-up plan. It included the extra amount needed to cover change-management and staff-hiring costs during the scale-up period. The executives who agreed to the plan expected to measure performance based on an average cost per item delivered (total costs divided by volumes). So they didn't want to separate these special costs as one-off project costs.

They were happy to spread these change costs across the overall volumes to get to their average cost, as usual. Experience told me that that approach would come back to bite us, because for two years our average costs would be higher than normal. But they agreed to the overall spend, so I bit my tongue and went along with it.

Sure enough, one year later, those same executives were asking why the average costs per item were not as they had expected. Every month the scale-up team had to explain in detail why the reported numbers looked the way they did. It was a painful reminder that the headline numbers matter most! Even if you have good reasons for them being different from what was expected.

CHECKLIST: BENEFITS OF SEPARATE CTB COSTS

- **Distinguish between running costs and growth costs**: Mixing these two means you will not easily see your "normal" operating costs or be able to confirm your profitability.

- Separating CTB costs gives you transparency on the **future viability of your business model** after your ramp-up is over. You can establish early in your ramp-up whether your BAU operating model is delivering the underlying costs to deliver your product or service as expected. This gives you more time to fix it if it's not right. If you lump all your costs together, it is difficult to distinguish true BAU operational costs.

- Managing your costs in different "run" and "change" buckets means you can **focus different leaders on each type of cost.** These activities require very different mindsets and skills to run well, so this is helpful.

- It's an excellent management discipline, which makes it easier to assign **individual accountability** for operational KPIs. (We'll cover KPIs in more detail in the next chapter, on People.)

- Of course, tech firms need to distinguish their **research and development** (R&D) costs, because in Australia you can get tax refunds for money spent on R&D. Many non-technology businesses capitalise their development costs on their balance sheet, so this makes sense for them too.

- Even when you're running a pilot at a small scale, it's worth breaking these costs into separate budgets. You will learn much more this way, all of which will be useful for the future scale-up.

ScaleCast Review: The Importance of Time

The pace of growth in most scale-ups drives very large swings in working capital. The way the business works and its financial profile changes dramatically while scaling up. So planning out the expected growth in detail on a monthly basis allows you to keep a handle on how this develops over time, which will have a big effect on the success of your scale-up.

The Cheque Is in the Mail

Let's start with an inconvenient truth: businesses cannot assume that everyone will pay them — or pay on time.

This explains why if you look around the world, you see so much focus on how to make sure small businesses get paid when they expect. The whole industry of "invoice financing", or factoring, builds on the need for small businesses to bridge the cash-flow gap between when they expect (and need) payment and when they do receive it.

Many reports published every year highlight slow payment as one of the biggest issues for smaller businesses, especially when the payment is coming from a bigger business. Accounting software firm Xero[16] claimed in early 2020 that 53% of all payments by larger businesses to smaller firms are paid late. Xero worked out that's AUD$115 billion per year, or $52,000 for each small business. That's a colossal amount.

My experience working with scale-ups and smaller businesses has shown this often to be true. I worked with one business that had an agreed contract with a global business and, despite providing services to it on time and to the agreed specification, the scale-up had to wait for payment, which ended up overdue by two months. The global customer explained this was because their internal sign-off procedures for the disbursement were held up by one of the approving executives being "busy on other matters". For the global customer it was a matter of an executive not having the time to wave through an agreed payment. For the scale-up, it was a matter of not being able to pay their staff that month if they didn't receive any cash inflow!

Moving at Different Speeds

The metabolic rate and the operating rhythm of small businesses are much higher than those of big businesses. Apart from the case of businesses paying small businesses later than they should, I have seen a big mismatch in expectations on how long it takes to get things agreed and done in big businesses. Scale-ups should plan for this, if they are relying on larger businesses to support their ramp-up plans in any way.

---

16. Reported in SmartCompany: "An Act of Business Bastardry" 7 April 2020. www.smartcompany.com.au

When I worked as a senior executive in a large bank, I had a friend (let's call him Roger) who was trying to get the major banks to take up a payments-related service his small business provided. It was a great product and the banks were all interested. But they took a very long time to review Roger's product and respond. He used to call me up for advice on how to get more traction with these bankers. I gave him every tip I could think of, but there was little anyone could do that would speed up the bank's internal processes. To be fair, highly-regulated, listed businesses like banks in Australia (and most other countries) will take their time because they have many internal hoops to go through, some of them imposed by external regulatory or legal requirements.

Roger got his purchase order in the end, 18 months later than he had hoped. This is a fairly typical experience for most small businesses.

This difference in operating rhythm can catch out scale-ups if they assume that they can push sales fast through the big business customer. To address this issue, I co-developed a course with the fintech hub Stone & Chalk in Sydney to help their scale-ups work out how to penetrate the bureaucracies of their big business customers. When we asked how long they thought it would take to "get to cash" — that is, get paid for their service — many assumed it would take 3 to 6 months. In reality, most would be strung along for 18 to 24 months by their big business customers, before getting contracts signed and first payments made.

My advice is to assume in your ScaleCast that it will take 18 months at least to bank revenues from a major business customer (especially if they are a financial services company). If you do get an eager, prompt-paying bank onboard, well done! *But take it as a lucky exception not the rule.*

CHECKLIST: TIMING EFFECTS ON YOUR SCALECAST

- Your ScaleCast does not replace any detailed cash flows you might need for financial reporting or management purposes. Keep your assumptions at high level, focus on when you expect the money to arrive in your bank account, and when you expect to have to pay the money out.

- **Document your expected "sales to cash" cycle:** Describe how long it takes to get from customer acquisition, to receiving the sales order, to the invoice (when the goods or service is provided), and to when the invoice is paid. *Allow a month between each step.* Assume there will be some drop off between these stages (i.e. not all acquired customers will make an order). Don't forget, some customers will not pay your invoice. You should record your assumptions about timing and drop-off for each stage in the cycle.

- **Pay attention to cash, not profit:** Note that for most businesses, the P&L account declares profit at the point where you invoice the sale, not when the invoice is paid and cash is in the bank — which may be much later. Your P&L could show you as going better than your cash balance in the bank. This is important when you're scaling up fast and self-funding your scale-up costs from sales cash flows.

- **Check your revenue-timing assumptions:** If your customer is a business, or you use other businesses as a channel to gain new customers, this is very important. You need to allow enough time to get from an "expression of interest" (EOI) to getting a term sheet out of that big business, to then getting a contract signed, the invoice accepted, and the invoice paid. If in doubt, err on the side of caution. Also, check the official terms of payment: some big businesses have a 60-days post-invoice term, not 30 days, so you need to make sure you take those things into account.

- **Consider seasonality of the business:** If business volumes change a lot because of weather or time of year, collect data and document your assumptions. It's important that you record what you're assuming. You need to ensure your model includes seasonal events (e.g. Easter, holiday periods) because they have a big impact on demand activity everywhere, including overseas. For example, if you have a business that's selling or purchasing from areas affected by events like Ramadan or Thanksgiving, you need to understand the impact on supply chains from a customer basis. You also need to check the supply side for the impact on your team capability. School holidays can affect availability of your staff, or service teams. Don't forget to consider the weather! If your business is sensitive to weather events, for example, the big storms in Victoria and New South Wales usually seen in December can have a big impact on the volumes of business coming into your scale-up.

- **Ensure your plan allows enough time to achieve scale-up prerequisites:** The starting point here is to review the Constraints and Capabilities you identified in the Strategy Compass session. For example, state licences can take months to complete if you're rolling out a national service. If staff are not easily available for hire in a particular state or market, you will need to allow extra lead-time (and maybe training) in your hiring schedule.

The Value of Experience

This exercise requires a mix of operational, financial and analytical thinking, and some expertise to get all of the less obvious points. The impact of time delays on your scale-up can be major. Even a few months could be costly, although you might not see this in advance when you're juggling as many issues as you will be in any scale-up.

It will be worth getting experienced advice from someone who has been through something similar, or at least knows well the areas or markets you are planning to expand into. This is also true for the last part of finalising your ScaleCast: a final check for any major mistakes or omissions.

Avoiding Errors and Omissions

It is possible to build a wonderful-looking plan that bears no resemblance to reality. There's only one thing worse than having no plan, and that's having a plan so wrong you cannot execute it. You'll destroy confidence (yours and your stakeholders), you'll end up spending a tremendous amount of time fixing the plan, and you still must drive your scale-up but without the benefit of a reliable roadmap.

So it's critical to "sense" check your ScaleCast once you've built it. "Common sense is not so common", as the French philosopher Voltaire said. It's easy to get so locked into the details of your plans, that you miss issues and challenges that will be apparent to someone less familiar with your business.

Confirmation Bias

Daniel Kahneman won a Nobel prize from his work looking at the danger of "confirmation bias", which describes how we pay attention to facts that support our beliefs, rather than those that challenge them. This seems to be hard-wired into all of us, and there are only two things we can do to help mitigate this, according to Kahneman and other experts:[17] look for data that disproves our conclusions; and enlist others with different viewpoints to review our plans.

It's very hard to challenge your own thinking. I recommend you encourage your team (and independent experts if you can get them) to challenge your assumptions and look at what happens if the assumptions are incorrect. This will also test your thinking around what are the important things you need to get right for the ScaleCast to succeed.

It's possible that you or your stakeholders think the facts are obvious, so any doubts on the plan will feel as if you are "second guessing" yourself. But it is the nature of scale-up change to bring new things into the business. Some of these will be unexpected, however smart you or your team may be. A bigger business is not just a small one multiplied a few times, so challenging your assumptions is never a waste of time.

Bearing these cognitive challenges in mind, let's look at what we can do to avoid the most common issues, errors and omissions. Think of them as **Golden Rules** that you should apply as a last check when you complete the first draft of your ScaleCast plan.

First Things First: Check Your Data

I'm hoping you have already double-checked your spreadsheet numbers (i.e. that they add up, or "cross cast" as they say). This may sound obvious, but I have seen some very important business cases re-written because formulas were copied across incorrectly, or not all the data cells got summed up into the totals. Sometimes the most basic issues can cause a problem: in one plan I was building we had half the numbers with Goods & Services Tax (GST) included, and half without. So we were off by 10% — a big gap over the entire business case!

Golden Rule: Check your numbers. Make sure they are all the same tax status (before or after), and that these assumptions are consistent throughout.

---

17. An interesting summary of this point is in Ben Yagoda's article in *The Atlantic*: "The Cognitive Biases Tricking Your Brain", September 2018.

CHECKLIST: TEST YOUR SCALECAST THINKING

- **Check that the Strategy Compass, SOAP and Shirt Sizing actually work in practice:** Your high-level assumptions can fall apart when you dig into the details. As you translate your assumptions into specifics by month, you can see where t makes little sense. Make sure you're not assuming perfect execution to land your scale-up. Always leave some room for error. For example, if you have a capacity of 100, you should not assume you will be at full 100% capacity all the time, because very few businesses work like that. Assume wastage, assume shrinkage (e.g. petty pilfering in a retail business).

- **Check that there are no "execution cliffs":** You'll see a "cliff you cannot climb" if the numbers in your growth plan go up month by month in a way that means you need to hire and train more people than you can handle. I have seen a case like this where we assumed we'd almost double the business in just two or three months — hundreds of people in total. You need to check that you're not expecting people to onboard when they're awaiting bonuses or on holiday. For example, to assume that you'll hire large numbers of people in December or January (in Australia) is unrealistic.

- **Performance and volume (P&V) test your operations:** This is something that IT companies talk about doing when they test their software on the production systems, to see if it can work at higher volumes and with more customers. You need to check that those new volumes fit — not only in your IT platform but also in your sales, operations, service, and financial systems. They need to be able to handle the increased volumes of people, product and service.

- **Look at outsourcing instead of doing it yourself:** Once you've got a service that's well defined, getting a service bureau (e.g. a call centre) to handle new volumes can deliver much lower costs at scale. It can also make your costs more variable too. See my earlier comments on "core v context", if you are not sure about which functions to consider outsourcing.

- **Check the business case works bottom up:** Is there enough cash to break-even? Are you making enough cash at the right time? Look at whether the reward — the return — is enough to justify the execution risk. For example, a net return (net profit margin) of less than 10% over time may not be too small, but the actual returns are likely to be smaller due to wastage etc.

- **Don't confuse P&L with cash flow:** The timing of sales, cash and non-cash items such as depreciation, and the timing of research and development grants, all have a different impact on the P&L than they do in your business bank account. It's important to separate profit from cash.

- **Don't assume perfection:** I've made many of the mistakes I've listed — and endured the pain of fixing them. For example, I built a scale-up case for execution that showed the resources needed to deliver the expected volumes of business at the required margins. I found that the finance department had taken the revenues and profit margins straight into their budget with no contingency, which meant they were expecting the best potential outcome (and no setbacks). It was a budget "designed for perfection", which like all budgets of that type was certain to disappoint the business stakeholders.

- **Review the sensitivities your business might have:** The bottom-line profits of some businesses are most sensitive to their customer conversion rate — the number of customers they convert into sales. Slight changes in these percentage rates can have a big impact on their profitability and growth rate. Other businesses might be more sensitive to the actual dollar value per sale. Others still could be sensitive to how long it takes for them to get sales through the system. Different business models will have different sensitivities, depending on several factors. Understanding how changes to your assumptions affect the viability of the ScaleCast is important. In one case I saw, it took six weeks to process work that was assumed would take four weeks. This delayed getting cash income by a month, and it meant the business needed 50% more people to process the work. It was a material change.

- **Consider whether your financials meet required minimums:** Although your focus will rightly remain on the P&L and cash-flow elements of your financial performance, in some scale-up businesses you will need certain amounts of capital or cash in tour business, to meet regulatory, client or financier requirements. For example, securing a building license as a company in Australia demands certain minimum capital levels in the balance sheet, and expected capital levels increase with volumes.

- **Check the contingency you have assumed in time and money:** Depending on the level of certainty in the business assumptions, always include contingency in your ScaleCast and your plan. It should include a contingency for both cost and revenue. You need to assume at least 10% impact across the business case (i.e. higher costs, lower revenues), and more where you don't know the market well. If you look at software planners, they will assume a 50% contingency when they start off doing their planning, plus or minus 50%. For this exercise, 10% sounds about right, but 20% plus may be appropriate, if you don't know a lot about where the market is. If your case needs contingency to be smaller than you first think in order for your sums to work, that's a red flag and the business case may not make sense in practice. *Don't build a ScaleCast that needs revenues or costs to hit their numbers exactly in order to be viable.*

Conclusion

The ScaleCast is at the heart of your scale-up execution plan. It needs to describe the key drivers of the new business well enough to allow your business to execute with success. Put aside the urge to dive into work ("let's get on with it") and avoid planning, because you find it boring or difficult. Nor should you delegate the plan to Finance — it's not just a budget or cash flow. You need to own this process so you can be sure you understand what's needed to make your scale-up plan a positive one, rather than an unworkable or non-viable one.

Always document your assumptions and manage different versions of your ScaleCast well. This is where version control becomes important. This may seem petty, but the fact is that you will not remember all the details a year later. It will save you confusion, error and a lot of wasted time as you go.

Next Steps

It's often said that an average strategy with excellent execution is always better than an excellent strategy with average execution! This is where the ScaleCast can really help.

Now that you've got your strategy ready for execution and described in your ScaleCast, you need to get your people lined up to deliver it. This is not always as easy as it first appears, and in the next chapter, we'll look at how to get that right.

CHAPTER 6
To Scale Well, Manage People Well

Every business, even the most high-tech businesses, depends on people to build and run it. Get the right people and manage them well, and you will have a strong foundation on which to scale well. In this chapter we'll look at the most important things to get right in people management to keep your scale-up on track.

This is not an HR professional's point of view. This is my perspective, based on three decades of line managing large numbers of people through all kinds of change, and observing and coaching others leading change.

What I know for sure is that you need to manage people in different ways, depending on where they are along the scale-up S-curve (see Chapter 2). In some key roles, you may need different people to run and grow your business than the people you have now, which can be an uncomfortable truth you have to face.

Often in smaller businesses I've seen a lack of structure around people management. This informality can be a strength when it allows agility and pace — but it can also be the cause of confusion, heartache and wasted effort across the business. This chapter will give you a structured approach and the tools to help you manage your people, which you can (and should) adapt to your specific needs and in line with the company culture you want to build.

"People Are Our Greatest Asset"

So many businesses fail to scale because they say "People are our greatest asset" without acting act like they believe it. They ignore the essentials that affect people selection, training and management.

Mediocre management of people becomes obvious in periods of rapid change. You can't hide when you need to move fast, do things differently and do things at scale. Keeping in mind three principles will put you ahead:

1. Be aware of the key success factors for managing people.
2. Avoid the people-related major mishaps that derail many businesses
3. Be prepared to make the hard people decisions <u>fast</u> to avoid longer-term pain or failure.

The large number of management books on this topic show that many business leaders realise they need to raise their game when the situation changes. These books range from *What Got You Here Won't Get You There,* which I referred to earlier in Chapter 1, to more specific change or growth focus works. The 2002 *Harvard Business Review* article by John Hamm on *Why Entrepreneurs Don't Scale* discusses founders who flounder.[18] These are executives who start a business or project that doesn't go well once they get the venture on its feet. Based on his work with over 100 entrepreneurs, Hamm found successful leaders are those who can jettison their old ways of doing things — and adapt their management approach to lead their organisations in different ways as they grow.

Venture capitalists look hard at the management team's capability, seeing it as a critical factor in the likely success of the scale-up business. In his April 2020 article *How Venture Capitalists Make Investment Choices,*[19] the author Ben McClure is blunt: "Quite simply, management is by far the most important factor that smart investors take into

---

18. Hamm highlights 4 key weaknesses for scale-up leaders: excessive loyalty to colleagues; task orientation; single-mindedness; and working in isolation. https://hbr.org/2002/12/why-entrepreneurs-dont-scale

19. https://www.investopedia.com/articles/financial-theory/11/how-venture-capitalists-make-investment-choices.asp

consideration. ***VCs invest in the management team and its ability to execute on a business plan first and foremost***" (emphasis added).

The People-Management Approach

Good leadership and good people management are important to the success of your scale-up. However, you probably don't have the time or the inclination to wade through all the available advice on managing people. Nonetheless, there are some key elements you <u>do</u> need to get right, which we're going to review in this chapter.

I've organised my comments around 4 domains, which are summarised in the People-Management Focus *(see Table 6.1)*. This simple framework is based on the principle that how you manage your people — and set the culture of your business — is shaped by **who** is in the business, and **what** they are tasked to do.

Table 6.1: People-management Focus

	Who	What
You	Your strengths and weaknesses	How you lead your team
Them	Get the right team, right job	How the team do their job

We will start by building a better understanding of who <u>you</u> are — your leadership style and experience — before looking at <u>how</u> you lead and manage the business, and <u>what</u> you should be doing to get the best results.

Then we will take a look at <u>who is in your team</u> — the people you have hired to help build the business, and then <u>what they do</u> to deliver against your expectations (and theirs!).

The interaction of these domains effectively creates the culture of the business you are leading. This culture will affect the way things are done, the engagement and energy levels of the team, and the resilience of the business to deal with the inevitable challenges that will arise during your scale-up journey.

Culture arises whether you plan it or not, and can be positive or negative, as you know from your own experience working in other businesses. The time that you dedicate to consciously design what your culture should look and feel like will be time well spent.

Culture is heavily influenced by the "tone from the top". So let's start by looking first at the leader of the business — you.

It's about You

Leaders are important to success in every business. The best leaders are self-aware about their personal leadership style, and how it drives what happens in their business, both good and bad. Leaders create the vision and energise their business with the passion and purpose they bring to that vision. It's this clarity and energy that allows leaders to bring their plan to life for their team, making the scale-up plan a reality.

The worst bosses can often be the best teachers. The worst, in this case, also means not self-aware. A few years ago, I worked for a leader like this — a CEO who liked to hire 'yes' people. He had great vision and was an excellent communicator but was undisciplined. He got bored with saying the same thing, so changed his key message every six months. The result was confusion, but this leader saw any feedback as unacceptable criticism unless it agreed with his view. The result was that his grand strategy failed. Eventually, a new leader was appointed who radically re-shaped the business and its strategy.

In smaller businesses, especially those going through rapid or large-scale change, leadership is critical. Deloitte research from 2015 on scale-ups[20] highlights **leadership experience and aptitude** as

---

20. *Scale-up: The Experience Game,* Deloitte Analytics, 2015. https://www2.deloitte.com/content/dam/Deloitte/nl/Documents/deloitte-analytics/deloitte-nl-data-analytics-onderzoeksrapport-scale-up-the-experience-game.pdf

key success factors in building "unicorns" — start-ups that scale to a market value of US$1 billion or more.

Closing the Johari Window

The pressure of change highlights and exaggerates the flaws and gaps in the capability of any leader. Those hidden features of yourself — invisible behind the Johari window I mentioned in Chapter 1 — can have an enormous impact. It's what you <u>don't know</u> about yourself that can create the biggest barriers to achieving your goals.

On the positive side, if you can get a better view of your gaps in knowledge or capability, you can either fix them or (faster still) compensate by hiring people strong in those areas.

You may think you and your management team are very strong and already have all the needed skills. Maybe you do. But in that case, you can use this exercise as a test to highlight the specific attributes you should look for in your new hires. My view is that there is always room to find out more about yourself in terms of your work personality and skills.

You might consider an evaluation tool such as a Myers-Briggs Type Indicator if you want to analyse your personality. However, if you first go through the exercises in this chapter, you will get the 80/20 view on the important attributes and attitudes for your scale-up. Think of it as a more focused and personal SWOT (your strengths, weakness, opportunities, and threats).

Approach: Completing the SGS Analysis

Table 6.2 provides a template for the **Strengths, Gaps, and Style** (SGS) questionnaire, which you can complete for yourself as leader, and (if relevant) your leadership team.

Each person should do this individually.

Table 6.2: SGS Questionnaire

Question	Rating (5 = high to 1 = low)	Weighting (5 = high to 1 = low)	Importance (Rating x Weight)	Action Steps
1. Experience – Functional				
Market/Industry	4	3	12	
Technology				
Financial				
People/Operations				
2. Experience – Scale				
Change Management				
Large/complex leadership				
3. Communication Preferences				
Listener or Talker	L = 5 to 1 = T			
Written to Oral	W = 5 to 1 = V			
Factual or persuasive	F = 5 to 1 = P			
4. Working Style				
Big picture or detailed	BP= 5 to 1 = D			
Decisive or fact-seeking	D = 5 to 1 = FS			
Starter or finisher	F = 5 to 1 = S			

Notes:

♦ Sections 1 & 2: Focus on areas with high importance (col. 4), then high weight (col. 3)

♦ Sections 3 & 4: Rating is to give preference (on a spectrum), not level of experience. Importance column not needed. Focus on specific actions to address any training needs.

If you have a team of leaders, compile that into an overall summary to look at strengths in your team that may cancel out the gaps in yourself or others.

It's hard to be objective about yourself. I suggest that you do it in teams with input from others that know you — or have this facilitated by a trusted advisor or coach if you are comfortable with that.

Follow these steps:

1. **Review** your SGS in at least the following four categories.

   - Experience — Functional

   - Experience — Scale

   - Communication Preferences

   - Working Style.

   Add short bullet-point evidence if relevant.

2. **Identify and weigh**

   - In this step, look back through your answers and describe the characteristics you see as being most critical for your success (and their relative importance).

   - Review plans you have to mitigate any gaps. For example:
     - training yourself or your leadership team
     - hiring specialists with those skills
     - employing advisors with relevant experience.

   - Once you've completed your SGS questionnaire, you'll be in a good place to look next at how to manage your team.

Before you are a leader, success is all about growing yourself. When you become a leader, success is all about growing others. So said Jack Welch, legendary CEO of GE in its pre-GFC heyday. In fact, it's as much about <u>how you lead</u> as how you grow your team.

It's about What You <u>Do</u> and <u>Say</u>

As a leader, you set the direction for the team (regardless of whether you intend to). In this section, we'll deal with the most important aspects of pointing your team in the right direction to deliver your scale-up. On the flip side, we'll also review the common leadership mistakes that you should avoid.

The Impact of Leadership

You'll know from experience how the tone of a business is set by the senior people in it — the way people talk to each other; the way they deal with tasks, issues and problems; how they manage themselves and others in good times, and through sticky patches. Although many scale-ups are non-hierarchical and more relaxed than traditional big businesses, the way the leadership thinks, talks and acts all have a big bearing on the culture and effectiveness of the team they lead.

Minor differences of approach can have a big impact over time. Think about an aeroplane taking off in Sydney and heading for Perth. One degree of change in its core setting will see the aeroplane slowly diverging from its original course until it ends up landing near Broome, thousands of kilometres away from its intended destination!

So if you're leading a big change over 18 to 24 months, everybody needs to understand where they are going. Leaders need to be consistent and have the same conversations with everyone. Even slight variations in message about where you're heading can have a big impact over time.

I saw this for myself when I led a major change program, during which I realised I was spending most of my time communicating upwards and outwards to key stakeholders. Meanwhile, the staff who were driving the change did not understand the big picture or even why some things happened the way they did. They were just doing what they were told to do, day by day. When I started communicating the broader story to the team, overall stress went down and team productivity went up.

Through this exercise, I found that many staff thought the scale-up state (i.e. constant change and considerable growing pains) was normal, and they didn't realise it was a transitional state. They needed to hear that when we got to the top of the S-curve, and reached full-scale operations, everything was going to settle down and feel much more stable.

Communicate Simply

As a leader, you have to communicate the right way, using language that's understood by everyone. Think of it like commanding a small army trying to capture an enemy hill. Your troops don't need to hear complicated explanations about what you're doing strategically to get ready for the battle — they need to know exactly what's needed for them to reach their objective. So, as a leader, you have to communicate not everything you <u>know</u>, but everything your troops <u>need to understand</u>. Only then can you be sure they'll know what to do, and how to do it without confusion.

It's not about "dumbing down" your message but checking for understanding and not assuming that everyone is always at the same level of knowledge. If you have new people joining you throughout your scale-up period (and it would be unusual if you didn't), then every new person has to come up the learning curve on what's going on, and why.

If you can communicate in terms that ensure everyone fully understands your key messages, you will immediately increase the effectiveness of your team.

Do We Really Need To Talk?

If you're used to working in a small business, you might assume that everybody knows what's going on. But this is almost never true once the business starts to grow.

In a start-up I worked in, early on with only 5 people in the office, there seemed to be no need to do any formal communications. But when we had an offsite after 6 months to recap where we were, it was clear that no-one on the team understood all of our scale-up story.

It can seem strange to run communications events or do formal communication planning when you've got a small team. But you do get bigger fast. If you build that habit of open communications early, it will be smoother and more natural to continue as you scale up.

In my experience, you can't "over-share" your leadership view of where the business is going, so that everyone remains well-aligned and on target.

It's the Way You Say It

The checklist below ensures that you communicate your leadership priorities and values clearly. However, it doesn't talk specifically about communication techniques (such as presentation style, tone of voice, or other more detailed points). Get training on these techniques if you or your leadership team are not comfortable with them.

The need for training or advice in this area is not a sign of weakness. It's about boosting your effectiveness on the job. If you can become clearer and more understandable as a result, the payoff for your scale-up team will be huge.

CHECKLIST: BEST PRACTICE FOR SETTING DIRECTION WITH YOUR TEAM

DO:

- **Create internal communications material:** Design it for talking through with the whole team, not just emailed out. It might be a presentation or talking points, but you're using it to get in front of the team and talk to them. *(See Table 6.3 for a suggested outline.)*

- **Ensure new staff have formal induction:** Tell new joiners about the business priorities and expected behaviours. If staff cannot attend induction sessions, make sure they have a one-to-one catch-up with the leadership team members on key messages. Getting new joiners on the same page as the original team maintains team cohesion and clarity.

- **Link strategic targets to individual and team KPIs:** It helps to align explicitly what people do day to day, and overall business targets. For example, you might have service quality or customer satisfaction as key strategic targets to drive growth. These should replicate onto the KPI measures of the individual team member, whose assessment will include how they have supported the overall customer satisfaction score.

- **Be honest about what you do and do not know**: If there's a lot of uncertainty in the scale-up, be honest about it. The worst thing you can do is pretend that you know something and then the staff realise that you're just talking rubbish. But if you don't know something important, make it clear what you're doing to find out and improve the position of the business.

DON'T:

- **Don't change the message:** It's OK to make some refinements, but not continuous changes to your strategic objectives or programs. When Jack Welch rolled out the

Six Sigma process-improvement approach across GE's hundreds of thousands of staff, he had to repeat the same message 50 or 60 times verbatim. He got bored saying the same things as he travelled around the world to present to staff. However, he realised that if he changed anything, he would give a different message to people hearing him for the first and only time. It's so important not to change the message once you've settled on your key strategy.

- **Don't be defensive about negative news:** If you find things aren't going right, you need to deal with the issue proactively, and communicate about it. We've all seen leaders who hate to give bad news, so they avoid being open. Teams prefer to hear the truth, and then to rally around to do what's needed to make things go better next time.

- **Don't let negative behaviour persist:** You can expect stress will arise in any major change activity. But bad teamwork has to be nipped in the bud. You need to deal with it quickly and show people that you won't tolerate poor or unhelpful behaviour; otherwise, you'll see cultural changes you won't like. If possible, you need to provide consequences to the person responsible and *make sure people know that you've dealt with it.*

- **Don't sound pessimistic:** Things may not be going well, but your team's productivity is linked to their confidence in the overall plan and in you. As a leader, even when you're not feeling great, you have to show confidence and realistic optimism. This doesn't mean you pretend to be happy or pretend that things are fine when you're not and they aren't, but that you always look on the positive side of any development. It means you are honest but also upbeat, even when the work is hard.

Table 6.3: Suggested Internal Communications Program

What	Content	Duration	When
Strategy Summary	High level purpose, approach and objectives explained. Focus on milestones and actions needed, including cultural goals.	30-45 mins	Annual (presentation)
Regular updates on how we are going	Informal progress v goals, "headlines & highlights"	15 mins	Every 2 weeks (stand-up, or phone call)
Email newsletter from Leader(s)	Summarising progress, key focus areas for team.	2 min read	Monthly (email)
Informal social gathering	Key message headlines, welcome new staff, celebrate birthdays and milestones	20 mins	Monthly (stand-up - "Morning Tea")
Social newsletter (OPTIONAL)	Profiles on new joiners, social events and team-building content. (Can also be included in 3 above)	3 min read	Monthly (email)

It's the Way You <u>Don't</u> Say It

Apart from the more explicit communication points covered above, do remember the impact of non-verbal communication. I can remember walking into an office with a toothache and people thinking something bad was happening because I looked so miserable! I had to explain I had a toothache. That made me realise just how closely teams watch their leaders.

There could be things happening in your life that have nothing to do with your work. But people look to you as a leader and expect you to be a barometer of whether or not things are going well. So it's important that you're clear in your non-verbal signalling, if you want to keep your team confident in overall progress to your shared goals.

It's about <u>Them</u>

You may have an outstanding founding team. But you need to find, hire, manage (and sometimes fire) a lot of new staff to make your scale-up work. Your ScaleCast will have helped you to identify many elements of the team you need. But when you're hiring new people, there are some key points that you should remember, and mistakes you need to avoid.

The bottom line for you is this: getting the people aspects of your scale-up wrong could be more painful for you *than anything else*. If you end up with the wrong people, or the wrong number of people, your scale-up is going to bog down badly. You will need to exert even more effort to fix the problems these people cause.

Right Job, Wrong Person

In every growth initiative I've led I've seen first-hand the impact of a job that outgrows the capability of the person who is doing it. Someone who did an outstanding job when the team was small can struggle when the business grows and they have to manage a larger team.

Once I had to build a team of banking operations experts quickly offshore, and the manager who set the office up and hired the team did it in record time. While he was great at getting things going, he was not good at managing people consistently and clearly over time. I needed to put a new manager into his role as the team grew in size, or it would have quickly become dysfunctional.

It's common to see good people not wanting to come onboard when you are in the pilot stage but getting interested as the momentum of the business becomes clear. I've found that the quality of candidates goes up as you grow. This means you can (and should) upgrade your original team members in order not to limit yourself to the ability of your "pilot-capable" team during your growth stage and at fu l scale.

The tech industry s littered with stories of founding teams that fell apart as their start-ups grew into multi-billion-dollar businesses. But beyond the headlines of founder fall-outs, many more people are hired, and then fired or sidelined, when their jobs become more than they can handle as the business scales up.

Unfortunately, people won't usually tell you that the job is beyond them. Sometimes pride won't let them; they used to be able to do the job, and it's hard for them to admit that now they cannot. Worse than this is where the individual is not aware that they are underperforming.

Meet Peter, the Chocolate Teapot

Some people retain an over-optimistic view of their own ability, despite consistent evidence to the contrary. Known as the *Dunning-Kruger effect* (named after the two academics who studied it[21]), it describes how low-performers often think they are more capable of doing a job than they are. At the same time, high-performers feel more anxious about their performance than they should. It's a good

---

21. Justin Kruger and David Dunning. "Unskilled and Unaware of It: How Difficulties in Recognizing One's Own Incompetence Lead to Inflated Self-Assessments." *Journal of Personality and Social Psychology*, 2000.

reason why self-evaluation can be deceptive! And why you should always take meaningful references before you hire someone.

Before I knew the technical term for it, I called this the "chocolate teapot" problem. People who looked good until they had to perform, when they would melt under the pressure.

In any business you will find people who are not capable, and who spend more time trying to look good rather than doing a good job. A long time before Dunning and Kruger, the management scientist Laurence Peter described the *Peter Principle*,[22] based on his observation of managers in big companies. He noted that they were promoted based on their success in previous jobs, until they reached a level of responsibility that exceeded their capability.

In a scale-up, you get the Peter Principle *in reverse.* Rather than employees rising through the company, the company quickly gets larger. Each job is now much bigger than before. For some people, it becomes a real challenge for them to succeed. They may have done an outstanding job at the start-up stage, but now they're struggling.

In one large scale-up I worked on, there were three lead managers who were all experts. They were solid people with great skills, but uncomfortable managing larger teams of people. As we grew, we moved them from being leaders of their functions into being trainers for hundreds of new joiners. They handed over their functional leadership to newly hired team managers, who had the experience to manage large teams. Team capability went up, and everybody was happy.

You need to handle these cases with compassion but also speed. Unlike the "chocolate teapots", these people will have helped the business in its early stages and may well suit other roles in the growing business. If you deal with these cases sensitively, it can reduce stress for everyone, and be a good thing for the re-deployed staff as much as for the business.

22. *The Peter Principle* (William Morrow and Company, 1969) by Dr Laurence Peter and Raymond Hull.

Applying Human Resources Best Practice

It's possible that by using HR best practice you'll be able to train your people to do a bigger job as the company grows. However, don't underestimate how unproductive people can be during a period of rapid change. Even with significant support and training, sometimes you will need to accept that not everyone is right for their scale-up role.

This doesn't mean you should ignore the need to adopt robust HR and recruitment planning approaches. At some point you will need specialised HR expertise, especially if you are hiring and training large numbers of employees.

The following checklist will help you focus as a leader on setting out the key priorities as you build the right team for your scale-up.

CHECKLIST: THE RIGHT TEAM

1. **Get the right staff for the right roles.**

   - Your ScaleCast should give you the basic numbers of staff you need.

   - Check your assumptions, especially around whether you need team leaders for larger groups or functional experts — for example, QA, IT, Security Compliance.

   - Check that the hiring and training assumptions are realistic, and whether you need any potential accreditation or validation. For example, do they need industry qualifications or any kind of prior experience?

   - Test your outsourcing options to increase the variability of costs and increase capacity. You may find it's faster, cheaper and simpler to have your service calls handled by an external call centre. If you do, remember that outsource options usually need more direction than it might seem. You cannot "outsource a problem" to get rid of it.

---

2. Manage poor performance decisively.

- Ensure formal performance contracts and probation periods are in use. This will help you deal with the "chocolate teapots" quickly and with as little fuss as possible.

- Assume turnover will be higher than normal within your scale-up, as roles outgrow some staff capabilities. Factor this into your hiring plans.

- Plan for and transition staff who have found their job has outgrown them, but who have exhibited good behaviour (i.e. positive, dedicated, and collaborative).

Diversity and Flexibility

As you build your team, it's natural to want to hire like-minded people, all dedicated to the same vision as you are. However, it's a good idea to check that your "A-team" is not <u>too</u> like-minded. You need diversity of thought across your team; otherwise you might miss something important in your scale-up plan. Different backgrounds, experience levels, and capabilities all bring something extra to the mix. A simple test here is whether your team ever challenges your thinking, or makes you consider issues from a different perspective. If the answer is no, you should consider broadening your team with more diverse members.

One way of coping with the need for a strong but diverse team is to be flexible on how you resource your business as you grow. You need dedicated team members in it for the long haul, but you should also consider using short-term contractors during your build period. Contractors can bring specific expertise needed only for a short time and can also help you avoid the "chocolate teapot" problem if you are not certain about your future needs in that function or role. It's critical that you are very clear on the scope, duration and objectives of the short-term role. This assignment can be amended if business needs change but being crystal clear upfront avoids getting lumbered with a "semi-permanent" and expensive team member who is neither fully in nor outside the business.

It's about What They Do

Growing from a small business to be a much larger one usually brings more complex people-management challenges. You will need to spend more time on managing people, and this is something that some leaders don't enjoy, and try to avoid.

However, it's always worth the effort: getting the right staff and managing them well will save a lot of your valuable time in the long run.

Once you have the right people on board, your priority is to ensure everyone does the right thing, in the right way. This starts as you onboard the team, all the way through the induction process, and into the nuts and bolts of how you manage them.

If you've managed people before, you might consider this as "People Management 101", which it is. But it's also good management of change. When you're dealing with people going through a lot of rapid change, you have to deal with the negatives as well as the positives. This means looking at what the stress of change can do to people, and how they deal with it.

Later on in this section we'll look at the "grief cycle". That may sound strange, but it is a useful model for thinking about how change affects people, and how best to lead them through the change process.

Management 101 — The Basics

Setting clear expectations around the EVP[23] — why they joined you — and the KPIs — what they should do — is critical. Expectations must be clearly stated to avoid misunderstandings, stress and wasted effort.

---

23. Employee Value Proposition — what the organisation offers its employees as a reason to work there; a key driver of attracting, engaging, and retaining talent. In short: What's In It For Them (WIIFT).

These basics will help you avoid people and performance issues that may otherwise hit you as you scale up.

MBO has long been a popular management discipline for setting goals and managing staff against them. As mentioned above, management guru Peter Drucker introduced the concept[24] to help managers set out what's needed from each employee, and the level of performance expected against each objective. Done well, MBO provides clarity and engages the team in hitting the business's strategic objectives.

Despite a long successful history for MBO in businesses of all sizes, many scale-ups seem to ignore this type of best practice in managing their people. Perhaps you might feel reluctant to focus so much on people management, seeing it only as a bureaucratic process best left to your HR advisor (if you have one).

I've observed that when you give people structure for their jobs and their performance, it makes the business more likely to succeed. Setting clear goals is an important part of your execution plan, and is a leadership responsibility, not HR. Scale-up leaders need to set the KPIs and expected behaviours, and then manage team members to deliver them. Team goals encourage collaboration, but it's important you also give recognition for individual performance, as well as coaching to each team member on areas needing improvement.

Many horror stories that I've heard from scale-ups come down to poor people-management processes. One business I joined for the purpose of helping them scale up seemed very cautious about my role. There was more oversight than I'd usually expect to see as an experienced manager. I later discovered my predecessor lasted less than six months and had been a total disaster. This person had bluffed their way into a leadership role but had no idea how to manage the team to deliver the scale-up objectives.

---

24. Peter Drucker, *The Practice of Management,* 1954.

Here are a few pointers for the most basic issues 've seen:

- When you're hiring people, **always take references**. Sometimes you find the only thing they could do well was sell themselves. Ideally, references should include a prior boss, and a previous direct report (or peer if they didn't manage anyone).
- Give people **detailed contracts and job descriptions**, otherwise you could end up in court arguing about responsibilities and why they didn't deliver them. I've seen ambiguous job descriptions lead to internal competition between two team members, who each thought the other was doing part of their job. If your company culture is so informal that a job description would feel odd, at least have a detailed discussion with the employee about your expectations — and theirs — and *summarise it in writing* (even if it's only an email).
- **Set public team KPIs:** Tell people the KPIs for the team and then cascade them down to individual team members. This makes it easier to align the team, and reward excellent versus average performance. All team members know how they are going individually, while collaboration across the team is also encouraged because everyone knows their shared goals.
- **Onboard employees professionally:** If you don't, you'll see a lot of turnover in good people who will not appreciate disorganisation as they arrive in the company. I've known new staff turn up and be unable to get access to their email for four weeks or more. That creates a terrible first impression, as well as making it harder for new employees to contribute quickly to your scale-up.
- **Manage change anxiety in your team**: If you see good people underperforming in major change, it can be because of anxiety or unfamiliarity with the change process. Deal with this first through listening to their concerns, then engaging to help them through the change, as we discuss below.

CHECKLIST: MANAGING YOUR STAFF THROUGH CHANGE

Follow the Before, During, and After model to help your team through the various stages of your scale-up journey.

BEFORE (before staff join you):

- Think about your **EVP**. Why would anyone who's good want to work for you? This could be as simple as a bullet list that you use for your job ads and interviews, but it should be genuine and aspirational. This is important. You need to write it down. Why would people want to join you? What is it they're joining you for? What do you offer?

- Create simple **written job descriptions,** focused on responsibility, scope of role and expected outcomes. Review them with people doing similar roles in your team to eliminate any role overlap or confusion.

- Always **take references** and any other **employment checks** you need — for example, police checks, licences and qualifications for particular skills. It's important to be thorough. In past roles, I've seen people send in forgeries when they're asked to confirm they have licences. No one in the past had ever asked them for proof of the real thing.

- Prepare a formal **staff onboarding and induction** process. It might include, for example, customer service training, orientation into the company and briefing on the company values and objectives. Include Health & Safety and other mandatory training and, if possible, do it online. This may seem excessive when you start with just a few people. But if you build a rhythm, you know that everyone has gone through the same process and is at the same stage when you get to the end of the scale-up.

- **Introduce new staff to existing teams**. When you have a large team, it can be daunting for new staff to introduce themselves to everyone. But building a sense of "being in this together" is important as you expand quickly. You can fast-track this by doing simple things such as regular newsletters with profiles and photos of new team members. I've also used monthly social get-togethers such as "morning teas" in different offices for people who've had a birthday that month or achieved something outstanding. Making sure your different teams interact and get to know each other can make a big difference to how things work when you're under pressure. Asking the team how they want to work together is always a good idea, as is setting out clear expectations on things like working from home and taking leave.

DURING (while people work in the business):

- **Publish KPIs** for the team and ensure every team member has an **individual scorecard**. In one scale-up we provided this online, updated daily with individual performance for our operators, most of whom loved the transparency. You should cascade those objectives down from the top. The objectives you have as a leader should flow through into individual targets. Not just the broader strategy, but also details of what you want in terms of things like hiring, getting customers onboard and getting sales. These should then flow through to each individual so they can see how their targets support the outcomes expected by their team leader.

- **Make KPI setting and tracking a simple process**. I have seen complex spreadsheets for 1% of effort here and 2% there, listing a multitude of target outcomes. I don't think that's easy to work to, and it is hard to administer. Individual KPIs should be three to five <u>key</u> objectives for each person, even if the business has many more things it wants to achieve. Goals must be meaningful, and something that the person can clearly deliver (i.e. not aspirational outcomes that depend on the efforts of many others).

- **Ensure that you differentiate performance**. Spell out and quantify what Fail, Perform and Outperform outcomes look like upfront. Of course, some elements or roles will be more subjective, such as in your compliance or HR team activities. Even in those cases, you should define what outstanding performance looks like. It's very demotivating for the team to go through performance evaluation and find out that their view of success is not the same as their manager's (or yours). It's also unhelpful if staff think that one team leader is an "easy marker" and their boss is tougher on them. *Fairness and objectivity have to be the key attributes of any evaluation system you put in place.*

- **Hold regular communications meetings** with all of the team members, at a team and functional level. Repeat your key messages across all levels of meetings. This may seem like a big call on your personal time, but it is well worth it. I have seen many mistakes happen in scale-ups, and things not happening that should, because people are not hearing the complete picture and getting the same messages.

- **Celebrate success!** Not just with big events, but a frequent combination of emails, call-outs, monthly morning teas, walking around and thanking people, "catching people doing the right thing" in the moment. It's a more important way to build morale than the year-end party or bonus. Those things might be nice, but people respond best when they're getting small and immediate recognition, rather than a year later.

- **Deal with performance issues quickly**: Ensure there is a probation period in your employment contracts, usually three to six months, during which you only have a one-week notice period. Pay close attention to your new team leaders, because if you have an underperforming team leader, they will weaken the performance of an entire team. It's hard to push people out when you're focusing on growth and opportunity, but it's something your people will expect and thank you for, and you will see the benefits in how the scale-up progresses.

AFTER (when staff are no longer with the business, from their choice or yours):

- **Exit staff professionally:** Many people decide for themselves that they're not up to the job. Make sure you have an exit checklist, equipment and data return list, access permissions to delete, and so on. Get simple signed release deeds confirming they have left the business and the terms under which they left.

- **Conduct exit interviews**: You might feel you're too busy for this but exit interviews can be the most valuable meetings you will hold. Staff will often tell you what they really think only when they're leaving the business. Cherish these comments — they will be valuable tips to fail-proof your scale-up, your management approach and the company's future. Some leavers will have a more negative view of your business than the general staff population, but what they tell you will be more helpful and honest than any staff survey.

Managing People through Change

Major change requires people to do things differently than before. Reviewing how you lead and manage people through change is an important part of your job.

When I first started work, it took me some time to realise this. But eventually I got it: *everybody deals with change differently.* The very first major project I worked on, many years ago, I thought everyone got as excited by change as I did. But it wasn't the case. I was talking about re-engineering and automating jobs that had been unchanged for decades. Most of the people doing those jobs came to work expecting to do the same thing every day, with as little change as possible. They might have grumbled a bit about things that were clunky, or processes that didn't make sense, but they felt settled in their work, and were not looking for upheaval.

So, as you can imagine, they were not happy with the major changes being proposed and resisted them. I was shocked, and then curious. It made me realise I needed to understand each person's preference for change, and which staff preferred job *certainty over job improvement.*

This wake-up call encouraged me to take a journey I'm still on: looking at how others manage change, and what we've learned about the best ways of managing people through change. There is almost as much material on change management as there is on business leadership! Academics have developed theories and best practice based on observations of leaders and organisations going through change. One of the most well-known is the Harvard Business School professor John Kotter. Over four decades he refined his now-famous eight-step change model[25] used by organisations looking to transform all around the world.

---

25. See https://www.kotterinc.com/8-steps-process-for-leading-change/

Kotter's model focuses on the leader who is introducing change into an existing environment. A scale-up is very different from a BAU organisation, but the need to manage the emotional aspects of the change is the same. In fact, it is even more critical. In a scale-up, where people join the team knowing they are jumping onto a rollercoaster, they will need help managing the personal impact of change, as well as the practical aspects we have covered elsewhere in this book.

Even in the middle of a major change, people always seek *certainty*. They want certainty about where the change is going, their role in it, and how to stay on track despite unexpected outcomes along the way. Even in fast-moving businesses, there are many who cheer change in public, but in private may be wondering: "Are we there yet?"

Managing these aspects of change well can stop your team crashing from emotional burnout and help them get to the top of the S-curve with positive energy remaining for the next challenge. One way that may help you frame this as a leader is to use a change model that focuses on managing the emotional side of change — the grief cycle.

The Grief Cycle Model of Change

It may seem strange to look at grief as an analogy for major change. I'm not suggesting that scaling up is going to mean that you and your team need counselling! But grief usually arises from a major change for the person involved — and the steps involved to deal with it also need handling in most other forms of major change.

The Kubler-Ross model[26] describes how people experiencing grief go through these five stages or emotions:

1. Denial
2. Anger
3. Bargaining
4. Depression
5. Acceptance

---

26. See https://en.wikipedia.org/wiki/Five_stages_of_grief

These are not always linear (taken in order), and they may not be present in every case. However, they do more or less describe the flow of emotions that occur to most people when something stressful or unwelcome happens to them. First of all, people think: "It's not happening to me." The second feeling is: "Why is it happening to me?" Then their third reaction is: "How can I make this less painful?" Next: "Oh no, it's happening to me." And finally: "Okay, it's happening. What do I do now?"

If change is being imposed on people, they may well go through this kind of cycle before they accept the new status quo.

Even the management team, and you as the leader, can go through this cycle, and this can represent a major leadership challenge. You need to consider the emotional impact on yourself from the scaling-up experience, which can affect you, your leadership and your team.

I've found that it helps to acknowledge the pace of change in your team, that the out-of-control feeling they've got is normal, and that it will not last forever. This gives everyone a way to work their way through the negative emotions they might be feeling, as they consider the personal impact on themselves from the amount of change your strategy demands.

It might seem corny, but in several scale-ups I have used a presentation that uses a picture of people hanging on for grim death as a rollercoaster plunges down its track. "Does it feel like this to you?" I ask. They always say: "Yes!". I explain the S-curve we are on and help them see that the way the business works will not feel like this forever. When we get to the top of the S-curve, it's going to feel very different. This kind of language talks to their emotional concerns, and helps the team manage themselves through what they are experiencing. This is an important part of a successful change.

Change Management Is Not Optional

The leaders of smaller, more agile businesses (such as most scale-ups) may not feel that people management is their comfort zone — that is, talking to people about their feelings. They may feel that neither the idea nor the practice of helping people change is their cup of tea. This is where many scale-ups with great strategies and business cases can fail to do well.

If this is not an area where you feel experienced or comfortable — and if your SGS analysis says it is a gap — then I recommend you get experienced help. It's going to help you manage your scale-up more effectively and reduce the risk of people burning out or becoming less effective from the emotional impact of change.

Unfortunately, it is not an area where there will be obvious flashing lights, or obvious targets to hit. It's one of those things that if not managed well will drag your performance down (as with other "soft skill" issues that affect the overall culture of your business). You need actively to look for it, to stop it becoming an issue, even if no-one is shouting about it to you.

Conclusion

People are a critical part of delivering a scale-up. Unless you manage them well, people-management issues can take your focus away from the other things you should work on.

HR teams and advisors can help you put a good people-management approach in place, but you have to own it and drive it as the scale-up leader. It will not be effective unless you and your leadership team treat it as important for success. You should build it into our ScaleCast plan alongside your more quantitative objectives and get some expertise on board if you don't have it yourself, to help you do this well.

Next Steps

Now you've got the people onboard and are well-positioned to deliver your scale-up strategy. But even great teams and great leaders need backing from outside the business. It's critical that your stakeholders are onside with what you're trying to do and how. In the next chapter, we'll cover what to do, and what not to do, to ensure this is the case.

CHAPTER 7
Managing Stakeholders

It's tempting to focus all of your attention and energy only on the business that you're trying to grow. But nothing happens in a vacuum. There are many important stakeholders that will be a critical part of your scale-up plan — the most obvious being investors. Your focus can't be only on building a "killer" funding pitch. It's also got to be on what happens after the funds arrive, when investors become shareholders and perhaps form a board.

This chapter is not about the investment pitch, although that can be a critical part of getting you through the "Valley of Death". There are a huge number of articles, books and even venture capitalists who can give you advice on this.

You may find a lot less written on why they would fire you or stop supporting you.

Who Are Your Stakeholders?

We'll be looking at three types of stakeholders:
1. The owners, which includes investors or a board, founders and employees with equity ownership.
2. Stakeholders who can help you — major customers, channel partners and major suppliers.
3. Stakeholders who can derail you — including regulators, banks, and the Australian Tax Office.

What Do Your Stakeholders Mean To You?

While stakeholders are important to your success, the decisions you make about them can have a significant effect on whether they are a positive or negative factor in your scale-up.

There are three kinds of decisions you need to make:

1. **Choosing your stakeholders.** You can't always choose them, but when you can, aim for the best fit. You need to work closely with them to achieve your goals, so need to be well-aligned, in terms of: **personality** (positive and professional), **value add** (experience and capability) and **alignment** (expectations and strategy).

2. **Your mindset**: how you deal with and react to them, especially in tough moments. Even when things are hard, managing yourself thoughtfully can make a big difference.

3. **How you communicate**: When? Through what medium? How open are you? This is the basis for empathy and understanding.

In this chapter we'll consider actionable steps you can take to ensure your stakeholders support your scale-up efforts rather than hold you back. We'll also consider *what stakeholders need from you* at the three different stages of change: before, during, and after. **Before** you start your growth phase, stakeholders will say, "Tell us what you will do for us". **During** scale-up, they will ask, "Are you doing what you said you would do and what you legally need to do?". **After** scale-up, they will say, "Show us you have done it as you promised".

Why Good Stakeholder Management Is So Important

Scale-ups represent dramatic change, opportunity and risk combined. Everyone affected by your scale-up plans will want to hear more about them. They need to see that you've thought about the impact on them, that you know what you're doing, and have a good chance of success.

If your plans don't convince the stakeholders, it can make things very difficult. There are many stories of boards and investors who fire the founder. One of the most famous examples is Steve Jobs at Apple. They fired him in 1985; he came back to Apple 12 years later, and then led the company through one of the greatest corporate resurrections of all time.

Although the Steve Jobs's second act at Apple is exceptional, many have lived through the first part of his experience, including me. I've led a scale-up through its planned ramp-up, but not kept the confidence of the board after my line manager left. This showed me how important it is to keep your key stakeholders comfortable with your plans, especially where the industry or market is new to them.

Continual communication and clear management of expectations are key factors in keeping your stakeholders onside. Those things were not good enough in my case, as I found out. Neither my direct-line manager nor the board understood the details of what we were doing. They saw the scale-up growth happening but didn't understand or like it when the immediate profits were different from what they were expecting.

If something doesn't meet expectations, this raises concerns about the competence of the jobholder. Stakeholders don't normally think this means they need to re-set their expectations or understanding.

These concerns and issues can affect any business. However, they are very important for a scale-up where rapid growth increases the pressures on all parties. So it's important to keep all the major stakeholders in your scale-up success onside.

Apart from the owners of the business, stakeholders include key staff, major suppliers, channel partners, and major customers. All have the leverage to pressure the business when cash is tight. They can also help you if they feel engaged and positive about the business direction.

You need to keep the regulators and your bankers onside. If you don't pay attention to these key compliance factors, it can cause real challenges and slow down progress. Issues here can also raise red flags amongst your other stakeholders about your competence as a manager.

Owners: or "Keeping the Boss Sweet"

Many small-business owners appear motivated by working for themselves, not someone else. This powerful theme appears in many online courses on setting up and running your own business, what's known as BYOB: Be Your Own Boss.[27] But unless you have an enormous pile of cash and can build your business funded by yourself, scaling-up your business will need support from Other People's Money (OPM).

This means you will have other owners or investors, either directly or through a board structure. This can also include other employees, co-founders and key staff you attract and reward with equity. If you scale-up your business, someone else in your business will expect you to "keep them sweet", even if they are not your day-to-day manager.

Choose Your "Boss" Well

When you're looking for funds to support your scale-up, or taking on a role leading a growth initiative, you may not be focused on how the investors or "owners" will shape your success. But this can be a crucial factor in your success.

Often scale-up leaders choose investors based on their convenience or availability; rather like having a quick and fancy wedding rather than a long and successful marriage. With the wrong approach to managing or choosing them, co-owners can become a huge barrier to success. If the goals of the stakeholders are misaligned with the founder's, they can also drive a scale-up off the road or eject the founder, based on their own attempts to minimise risk to their investments.

In late 2019, the US research firm CB Insights published a review of start-up failures.[28] This review identified investor or team dysfunction as a major cause of failure in over one hundred

---

27. For example, see https://www.latrobe.edu.au/nest/employee-entrepreneur-become-boss/
28. https://www.cbinsights.com/research/startup-failure-reasons-top/

cases they examined. Among the top reasons for failure, 25% were attributed to not having the right team, or the lack of a co-founder with the right skills; 40% of the start-ups failed because of no market need for their service or product.

To launch a scale-up without an identified market need suggests an enormous failure in oversight by the investor group. You would expect the board to identify that fact, either by shutting down the scale-up or pivoting to meet a real market need.

Many articles describe how a business should select a good investor.[29] It's not just about having deep pockets, or a big brand and business connections, but about "soft skills" to help guide the business.

The number-one skill identified was *how the investor interacted* with the business they put money into. *Operational know-how* was the second-most important skill: how to help the scale-up be more effective. Third was *industry knowledge* — ensuring the business maximised its opportunities. These attributes are all about the investor bringing not just money, but also valuable experience to help the scale-up.

The Value of Choice

You might find that you don't have a choice over who your investors or board members are. Maybe they're a corporate sponsor, or a major customer is a funder, or you're funding it with family and friends. That may work out well for you — but if they don't work out, your "boss" — by which I mean board, investors or co-owners — will disrupt your scale-up, whatever the ownership structure.

Back in the 1990s, I launched online banking as a service for the customers of a major UK bank. The project was owned and managed by the Consumer Banking department, which appointed me to lead the team. The IT department, which we considered a major sponsor, reacted badly because the approach we took was different from what they were

---

29. For example: https://www.forbes.com/sites/alejandrocremades/2018/12/11/how-to-find-the-right-vc-for-your-startup/#39a5129188f2; and https://bothsidesofthetable.com/what-i-would-look-for-when-choosing-a-vc-knowing-what-i-know-now-fbdc67689449

used to. They were not used to non-centralised and accessible systems in the mid-1990s. Just after we launched the service, accountability for my business department transferred to the IT department, as part of a bigger company re-organisation. My new bosses changed all of the management, including me, despite the service having won plaudits and many tens of thousands of clients. There was no alignment between what the IT bosses expected and what we were doing, and that was a major problem for them (and us). The IT department started out as a key stakeholder and then they were put in charge.

This experience showed me you need to work hard to keep all of your key stakeholders onside, even where their perspectives might differ from your own. Stakeholders today may be bosses tomorrow, especially where your scale-up is part of a bigger corporate initiative. You may not have any choice over these changes, but you can still apply the tests. This will make it clear how you should manage these "involuntary" owners for the best.

If there are other co-founders or equity-holding employees, you want them also to pass the tests I mentioned at the start. Many new businesses are disrupted by these issues. It's a source of strength when everyone's aligned, and a significant problem if they're not.

CHECKLIST: CHOOSING (AND MANAGING THE RIGHT OWNERS)

1. Always explore your options. Don't take the first volunteer who's providing money. Think about:

   - **What funding do you need and for how long?** Your ScaleCast should give you a definite view on this. Who could provide funding that would be a good fit?

   - **What expertise are you lacking that you need to fill —** either through internal staff or through external advisors, including venture capitalists?

- **What equity do you need to share with your existing co-founders?** On what basis? Keep their interests in mind as you make this decision.

2. Build a long list of 5 to 10 potential sources of funding and test them against your 3 key assessment criteria: **personality, value-add,** and **alignment**. Rank them on a scale of one to five if possible. Do the same when you're considering employee equity holders.

3. **Adopt and plan communication approaches** for weekly, monthly, formal, informal, written, and face-to-face methods. Decide how you will keep them up to speed with what you're doing. *Ask them how they would like you to communicate with them!*

4. **Review your owner communications** on at least a quarterly basis. As your business scales up and changes, the communication needs of both you and your owners will change. Don't brief over coffee when you need to be presenting to the board. Check-in with them on what details they need to see, which may well change.

5. **Consider your attitude** and check you are being positive and empathetic to their needs. If possible, get feedback from a trusted advisor or insider on the board or ownership group. Believing they're wrong-headed when they challenge you won't help. If you react badly, it will weaken their confidence in you, even if most other things are working well.

What If You Have No Choice?

Several factors may divert you from best practice. Pressure to get funding quickly can make you want to take the first offer that meets your cash-flow needs. You may worry that using formal evaluation criteria may put off some venture capitalists or owners.

My advice is you should always try to take the "one-year view": *How will you feel in a year's time about the deal you are looking to strike?* If you can manage your cash flow to give you the time to make an informed choice, this will help you discriminate between potential owners based on the best fit with you and your plans, not on availability of cash. It will remove potential issues arising from misalignment of interests, as you continue to scale-up.

Major Business Partners: Enablers or Disruptors?

Many scale-ups enlist a major business partner as a sponsor, paying for the service directly or as a channel to market. They're not owners, but they still expect to be treated as insiders, more than a normal commercial arrangement.

Major business partners have ambitions and expectations that won't always align with your scale-up plans. They may represent 100% of your business at the beginning, but *you are* a *tiny percentage of theirs*. This asymmetry in bargaining power between you will show in their expectations of you.

Take, for example, a big bank working with a small fintech. The bank has different interests from the smaller business. If you don't treat this with care, business partners like this can derail your scale-up. The bank may pull the plug if they change their strategy, because of internal politics or a change in business priorities. Your profitability may be affected if they insist on difficult terms and conditions. They may slow down the scale-up to mitigate their own risks, or they may limit the upside of the scale-up, if they insist on exclusivity through tough contractual terms.

On the positive side, major business partners can speed up time to market, reduce customer acquisition costs and help you close capability gaps in your business. They can also help you manage competitor activity.

Managing these major partners well can make or break your growth plans. Understand them and keep them positive about you; it's a key requirement to keep your scale-up safely on track.

The Importance of Major Business Partners

A large number of articles on channel-partner management describe how major businesses are used as a channel to market by smaller businesses. A quick web search will show you the usual range of management behaviour by channel partners, from good to poor.

The channel partner-specific news website CRN[30] highlights how poor alignment between a vendor and their channel partners leads to problems. **Channel conflict** arises where you're trying to sell something and your channel partner wants to sell it in a different way or for a different price. That may lead to issues around how and when sales happen, and differences in expectations on reward and effort. Channel conflict can arise in just about every kind of business industry.

With all these potential issues, why use channel partners at all? Often you have little choice if you want to enter a market fast. Despite the potential pitfalls, if you manage your channel partners and suppliers well, they can make your scale-up go faster, as they will shoulder much of the load of getting to market.

Even where you sell directly to consumers, partner support can be important to help you sell, service or supply your offering. Don't ignore the scale-up opportunities in building an effective relationship with those potential stakeholders.

Building Trust and Alignment with Business Partners

It can take a considerable amount of agility, forbearance and effort to develop a strong relationship with a key business partner, but the value of these relationships can make or break the scale-up.

Let's consider two examples to illustrate the complexity of these cases.

---

30. https://www.crn.com.au/feature/channel-partners-biggest-annoyances-with-vendors-468635

A. The Major Customer Becomes Too Interested

Joe* won a key international bank contract for his software as a service (SAAS) scale-up. After two years of piloting the proof of concept, he got a regional contract and was rolling it out across Asian countries with a global contract on offer. The bank also wanted to invest in his business.

Despite excellent progress, the bank was slow to pay him, and continued turnover in the executive ranks meant that Joe and his team needed a huge effort to keep them onside. Sponsorship had been won from the bank's global functional heads, due to the enormous value of the software service to the bank. Joe had the opportunity to break even on his costs and accelerate his growth. After patiently working his way through the bureaucracy and their slowness in paying bills, continued growth was Joe's reward. His challenge now was to build new business while continuing to service a major client and avoiding becoming a captive supplier to just this bank.

The bank venture capital division offered to take a stake and inject capital for him, but this might have deterred other banks from becoming customers. By considering fit and what he would do in future, he avoided getting embedded too closely with the bank venture arm in order to make sure that he continued to grow beyond this one customer.

B. The Major Supplier Supports the Business

Tom* is the CEO of a distributor of overseas products manufactured in Europe who built up a personal relationship with the CEO of a major supplier. He even hosted the supplier CEO's adult son in a development role in his business for a year in Australia.

Because of this good relationship, the supplier extended credit terms for shipment payments. The supplier also

---

* Names and details are altered to protect the privacy of those involved.

supported Tom through slow sales periods, including the coronavirus lockdown in 2020. Over time it became a very strong relationship and a major support in growing and maintaining Tom's business.

CHECKLIST: MANAGING YOUR MAJOR PARTNERS

1. **Identify** your major channel or supply stakeholders to support your scale-up. Review your Strategy Compass for pointers on Supply and also Customer.

2. **Assume some drop-outs**. Establish more capacity than you think you need, in case your original partner or supplier cannot deliver the expected volumes as you grow. Don't assume that one major supplier, or one major channel partner, is the only answer. You need to make sure you've got other options.

3. **Review your key stakeholders** against your assessment criteria: Personality, Value-add and Alignment. *Rank them on a scale of 1–5 if possible.*

4. **Plan your engagement** with them. Decide who in your business manages that relationship. Treat it like a sales call, with the target being to improve communication, trust, and alignment of objectives. *Aim to improve your rank score out of five after every contact.*

5. **Continue to review** your key channel partner and supplier stakeholders each quarter. As your business scales up and changes, your partner and supplier needs will change. You need to flag this and check your partners will support you before you get to the crunch point. *Don't find out they can't help you just as you commit to an all-out expansion.*

Keep Partners Close

Managing channel partners and major suppliers well can make or break any business. That's why bigger businesses spend time and money on it and hire specialist managers to ensure it's done as well as possible. For your scale-up, it can also be a critical area to get right.

Planning in detail what you do with these major stakeholders might seem onerous. But getting it right from the outset and building strong relationships (without becoming "captive" to a major supplier or partner) will pay off when you need it. From financial support to great positioning as a preferred channel supplier, the upsides can be large. The downsides of falling out with these stakeholders can also be significant. When suppliers are less helpful and demand payment upfront, for example, almost every business will feel the pain.

Compliance Stakeholders: "Business Prevention Squad"

For every business, however innovative you might be, there will be rules you need to follow. There are always regulations, laws, or industry best practice that you must obey in order not to get bogged down in a swamp of paperwork or litigation. Comply with what's expected, even if you feel this is stopping you getting on with your business. You may feel that the people or functions overseeing these compliance requirements should call themselves "business prevention officers"! But they are there for a reason, and you must not relegate them to an afterthought.

Compliance stakeholders are different from other types of stakeholders, but they're important. If you don't get this right, your scale-up may come off the rails. You should ensure legal, compliance, health and safety, and other specialists are on tap for advice, but you can't abdicate responsibility to them. The buck always stops with the most senior leaders n a business.

This May Be You

Many scale-up leaders will believe they are not large enough to worry about regulators. But the "trickle-down" effect of regulation is already happening, and several businesses have become unstuck because of poor advice. If your business fails to do something that's legally required, you're in the frame as the CEO or a business leader, not the advisor.

Let's look at one major example of leaders taking responsibility for compliance breaches rather than their advisors. Multi-billion-dollar property business Centro Group published inaccurate financial statements in 2007. The board relied on management and auditors to get their financial statements right. But the board was sued by its regulator, the Australian Securities and Investments Commission (ASIC), in 2011 for breach of its duties under the Corporations Act. The directors were declared liable, the CEO was fined $30,000, and the adverse findings impacted senior careers, on top of the stress of four years of legal proceedings.

The 2018 Hayne Royal Commission saw senior management of large financial services businesses lambasted for their failure to follow expected rules, and their inability to explain their conduct to the Commission. Legislation passed in Australia (and around the world) over the past decade has tightened the focus on executive responsibility and heightened the expectation that businesses will always follow the rules and regulations.

The conduct of major businesses is the focus of regulations such as the Business Executive Accountability Regime (BEAR) for larger financial institutions in Australia, and the banking regulator APRA's[31] prudential standards on outsourcing (CPS231), information security (CPS234) and managing data risk (CPS235), which all specify

---

31. The Australian Prudential Regulatory Authority (APRA) issues prudential standards that regulated entities are required to follow. These cover a wide range of topics, from financial, capital and economic requirements, through to themes of general governance and risk management. Regulated entities need to show they are compliant on a regular basis, and if APRA is not satisfied that they are, it can impose sanctions that extend to withdrawing the business's operating licence.

how banks should manage themselves. Regulation on these larger businesses has in turn led to rising expectations on fintechs and other suppliers to the "top end of town".

Legislation like the *Modern Slavery Act 2018* (Cwlth) requires businesses to confirm that neither they nor their suppliers exploit employees — for example, by paying them less than the minimum wage. In a scale-up I worked in, we had to confirm (through a legally binding statement) that we had complied with legislation aimed at the major business we supported. If we had not confirmed our legal compliance, our scale-up with that major business would have come to an immediate stop.

Fire Prevention, Not Firefighting

The principle behind good compliance is fire prevention, not firefighting. It's good to have leaders who can respond well to crises, but it's even better if you're organised so that the crises don't arise in the first place.

Regulators always get more positive about a business where they can see that senior managers are taking their responsibilities seriously, rather than passing them off to juniors or specialists to run with.

So you need to pay attention to the regulators for your scale-up market. They will drive your expected behaviour directly, or via the major businesses acting as your customers, channel partners or suppliers. In addition, there are other compliance stakeholders that need to be well-managed:

- **Tax officers** expect and demand full compliance with all tax laws. They're almost always a preferential creditor (in a winding-up situation), so they have enormous legal and practical power. They're also the source of refunds for R&D investment. Make sure your PAYG (pay as you go), GST (goods and services tax) and superannuation arrangements are all sorted out, if you are hiring lots of staff fast.

- **Health, safety and environmental (HSE)** requirements can be a major issue for businesses such as building or trades. The HSE regulator WorkSafe can shut down an office or other business operation it deems unsafe.
- You'll need **insurance** for your business, public liability indemnity (PLI) as a minimum, but also general insurance for premises and equipment, and this might extend to cyber-security insurance to protect your business from disruption or loss caused by hackers.

Many small businesses adopt a bare minimum approach to many of these areas. If you're running a scale-up, this means that you will have to do a lot of process redesign and introduce new management controls, after the business has already grown. It's difficult to get people to change and add extra controls once you've scaled up. It's far better to build a compliant operation from the start, in partnership with health and safety and compliance teams and in line with legal expectations.

CHECKLIST: COMPLIANCE STAKEHOLDERS

1. **Identify the required** licences and compliance regimes that your business needs to follow, based on its industry and activities. Start with the Australian Business Licence Service: its website at https://ablis.business.gov.au offers a useful online guided search tool.

2. **Identify the functional stakeholders** who will support or keep safe your business. This includes your bank and accountant. You may have R&D grant specialists or Export and Marketing Development Grants (EMDG) specialists, a lawyer, an IP or patent lawyer, or an HSE specialist needed.

WorkSafe is also usually relevant. You may also need a specialist in compliance checking, to confirm operating licences needed by your staff and your business.

3. **Build a simple management summary** of your status with each of those key compliance stakeholders, including actions that you need and those that are outstanding. Who owns the action in your management team? It should be you or one of the senior leadership team.

4. **Review progress** with your management team monthly. Get input from your trusted advisors on any obvious omissions or errors. Take action when there are gaps or issues identified.

5. **Review all of this against your scale-up plan**, including your expected arrival point — the point at which you will have reached full scale, where the pace of change and growth has finished. That will be 18–24 months after you start your scale-up in most cases.

6. **Consider hiring a full-time compliance lead** — for example, legal counsel or a head of compliance or a head of health and safety. If you think you need them, hire them early, if possible. Try to hire action analysts — problem solvers, not problem spotters. That way they'll be scale-up enablers and not business preventers. It can take a lot of time to find specialists who fit with you and your culture. Interim or internal specialists can help bridge that gap. Make sure this is not a tick-box role around giving advice that people like yourself then ignore, because when it matters, it will really matter.

Get the Right Advice

Banks and specialist advisors, such as lawyers, accountants, and patent attorneys, can be very helpful when you're under pressure, so keep them onside. Planning well ahead is always good practice.

Being professional and open is important, not leaving things to the last minute and then asking for help.

It's very important to choose the right advisors for you. If you haven't chosen your advisors well, your scale-up can suffer from either too much legal caution or be too exposed when entering new markets. I worked with one entrepreneur who had filed patents to protect their IP. But over 18 months, their patent attorney advised them they should have filed patents in major markets around the world. It cost them hundreds of thousands of dollars for very little business benefit. At the very least, be careful about who you trust to advise you on some of these legal or other compliance requirements.

You may want to consider appointing an Advisory Board for your business — in which case, read the information below.

ADVISORY BOARDS

Advisory Boards are common practice in the non-profit sector and have become increasingly popular in SMEs and scale-up businesses.

Unlike a company's Board of Directors, which has legally defined responsibilities and represents the shareholders, the Advisory Board is an informal group of expert advisors chosen by the CEO and management team to help them. It has no legal standing or accountability for business performance, and therefore can only advise and not govern.

Your Advisory Board is an informal but structured part of your business, usually with a nominated chair and regular members who hold meetings several times a year, on topics of strategic importance to the business. The size of the board, frequency and agenda of meetings, and tenure of advisors can all be set by your needs and those of the business. It can usefully provide skills and expertise, as well as a "sounding

---

board" for you, without confusing this advice with governance issues that are the preserve of the company board.

The main benefit of an Advisory Board over individual advisors is the power of collective problem-solving it provides when you're facing major issues or opportunities. Used well, the Advisory Board can complement areas of inexperience in the leadership team, as well as providing a "think tank" when needed to help management clarify thinking and strategy.

If you want to find more out about this subject, a good source of information and best-practice guidance can be found at www.advisoryboardcentre.com.au.

You may find it helpful to join a scale-up community — known as an accelerator or hub — such as Stone & Chalk. There you can learn from other scale-up leaders and mentors who are usually happy to share the benefit of their experience, often on a pro-bono basis.

Compliance is a specialist function. If your industry requires certain forms of compliance, other members of your team can do specific things like run police checks on new staff — but it's you, the leader, who needs to make sure that your business is compliant. The best way to make this work safely is to pay attention to the details, to ensure that your business is following all of the relevant regulations.

Conclusion

Stakeholders outside the business will have an enormous impact on whether or not your scale-up succeeds. Treat them right and they will make everything work smoothly. Get it wrong and they'll make your scale-up a nightmare.

I can almost guarantee that you will be tempted to wing it for some of the less exciting elements of stakeholder management. There's always more exciting stuff to do than manage licences and compliance! But one secret of getting to scale is having a recipe to take you through the boring but necessary bits. If you overlook them, they might bite you somewhere painful! Ensure you have all of your stakeholders identified, well-managed, fully engaged and supportive of your scale-up business.

Next Steps

This chapter has focused on managing risks and issues with stakeholders. Next we'll look at the broader risks that arise as you scale up your business, and how you should manage them effectively: what can you do when things don't work out as you hoped they would?

CHAPTER 8
Risky Business – Managing Scale-Up Risks

All change brings risk. Management guru Peter Drucker once said, *Whenever you see a successful business, someone once made a courageous decision.* If you're thinking about scaling up your business, you're already in a minority in terms of your appetite for risk. But success is not just about <u>taking</u> risks. It's about <u>managing</u> risks well before they become issues. Issues are risks that have become reality; they are now problems you have to deal with. In this chapter, we'll cover the difference between real and theoretical risk management, and how to avoid failure and unnecessary paperwork.

Are You Paying Attention?

I have to confess that risk management is not the most exciting topic to talk about. I'm fairly certain you're reading this because you feel you have to, not because you expect it to be a wild, fun ride.

If you're a founder or scale-up leader, you will find risk management boring and procedural. It's going to send you off to sleep — right up to the moment that a fire burns down your premises and you have no plan on how to get your team back on track. Or you realise your customers see you as a potential risk to their success, and you need to prove that you aren't.

Managing risk well is essential. It lets you dodge the bullets you should see coming. It also allows you to reassure your stakeholders in ways they understand and allows you to get more business from your customers when they see that you are a well-managed business. Understanding and managing your risks well will save you time, cash burn, and wasted opportunities.

Good risk management is also important to run the business better at scale, as we'll discuss in the next chapter.

What's So Important about Risk Management?

It's rare to find Mark Zuckerberg and the Dalai Lama (mostly) in agreement:

> *"The biggest risk is not taking any risk. In a world that is changing really quickly, the only strategy that is guaranteed to fail is not taking risks."*
> *— Mark Zuckerberg.*

> *"Great love and the great achievements involve great risks."*
> *— the Dalai Lama.*

Scaling up a business means taking big risks. You know that. Even well-established businesses focused on strong risk management can get it wrong. Many of the bad-news stories about big banks in Australia, and elsewhere over the years, have in large part been down to poor management of risk. Not credit risk, which is about banks losing money, but operational reputation risk, which is something every business (including yours) needs to get right.

In response to this history of operational risk problems, every bank has invested a lot to beef up their risk management functions. The governance, risk and compliance (GRC) profession has become one of the few growth sectors within banking, with tens of thousands of new roles created in banks worldwide.

There's also been tremendous growth in innovation businesses providing regulatory technology, or "Regtech", a fast-growing sub-set of the high-flying fintech industry. Risk is a booming business.

Our Approach

Let's be clear: we've already covered many of the "usual" risks arising from scaling up your business in earlier chapters. That's what the "Scale without Fail" method is all about. We have looked at how risk is well-managed in major businesses, and what you can use from this to "de-risk" your scale-up plans.

So our approach in this chapter focuses on risk **awareness, mindset** and **approach.**

We'll look at those three parts in more detail:

- We'll start with the **Risk Profile** of your scale-up — where are you now?
- Next we'll cover **Risk Management 101** — the simplified theory.
- Then we'll look at **Regulator Risk** and what regulators and stakeholders think.

We'll wrap up by looking at **what you should avoid in managing risk** in your scale-up.

Risky You — Your Changing Risk Profile

Risk for your scale-up develops and changes as your business grows. This is true for every business, but it's very significant for a rapid-growth business. You need to adjust your aim and keep your focus on those risks that need attention at that stage.

Building good risk management habits early on will help you as your business grows, and what's at stake gets bigger. You can implement risk management habits and processes early on that need not change much as you grow. However, the specific risks you must manage <u>will</u> change: for example, as you grow, who you hire and their ability to do their jobs becomes a more important business risk. You will need to work out ways to manage this, ahead of time.

Back to the S-Curve

If you look at the S-curve diagram *(see Figure 8.1)*, you'll see business risks specific to each stage of the business's lifecycle.

A good perspective on the risk of scale-up at each stage comes from the professional investor or venture capitalist (VC). The VC will understand the likely *future value* (FV), in dollar terms, of the business when it gets to full scale, and this view of FV should be mostly the same at each funding stage. However, the *present value* (PV) at which the VC will put money into the business at each fund-raising stage will change. As the business moves through the various stages of growth, from pilot all the way to full roll-out, the VC will consider that execution risk is declining, and the FV of the business is becoming more certain. So the VC will discount the FV by less and assign a higher PV to the business.

Scale-ups that follow the usual growth stages start in the pilot or prototype phase, where the major risk is inability to prove the viability of the business model. In the Scale phase, the major question (or risk) to answer is whether the scale-up can deliver growth fast and safely. As the business gets to full scale, risks centre on the sustainable profitability, reliability and safety of the business. We'll cover the major elements of this last stage (Stabilise) in more detail in the next chapter.

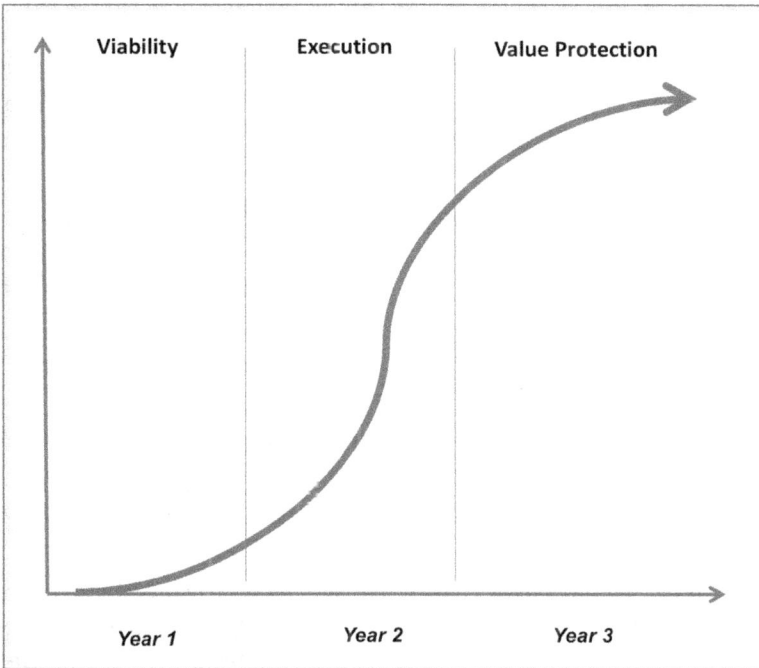

Risk By Stage

Year 1 – Viability	· Is it worth it?
	· Can **you** build it?
Year 2 – Growth	· Can you grow safely?
	· Can you validate the business model in practice?
Year 3 – Operational	· Can you run the business safely at scale?
	· Are compliance, legal, other aspects well-managed?

Figure 8.1: Lifecycle of Risk

Guessing the Unknown

Perhaps your business is so novel that there are few guides to how it's going to go, and you feel this makes it hard to describe risks in detail.

157

I have some sympathy with this view. New risks and issues will emerge as you scale up, and not all of them will be foreseeable. I don't think you should craft detailed "what if?" scenarios either, as these are unlikely to drive much useful action, but may confuse or scare yourself and your stakeholders!

However, I <u>do</u> think it's possible to identify the major risks most likely to arise and outline them at the outset. You need not manage them until they're relevant: you have to get out of your MVP stage

---

CHECKLIST: REVIEW YOUR RISK PROFILE

1. **Review the major outcomes you are expecting**. The work you have done to compile your SOAP and Strategy Compass should give you an excellent idea of these major deliverables.

2. **List the major risks** that you might need to consider in order to achieve your outcomes. As an aid, *Table 8.1* provides a number of potential risks you might want to consider, using the lifecycle stages (Start, Scale, Stabilise), the 5P framework, and the 4 points of the Strategy Compass.

3. **Customise the general risks to the specifics of your business** and remember the 80/20 Rule: not everything but include all of the "big rocks".

---

before you worry too much about execution risks, for example. However, tracking these risks and mitigating their impact on you will mean you avoid major issues with a bit of planning.

The first step is to look at your own risk profile, before we consider a simple approach to managing these risks as you grow.

Not all risks will be apparent at the outset. That's okay. As you know, the rule is iterate, iterate, iterate! You'll be able to revise this list of risks during our review in the next section.

Table 8.1: Potential Risks Pick List

Lifecyle Stage	5P Framework	Strategy Compass
Start Business model IP MVP Capability to launch Funding	**P&L** Finance (funding) Business Model Market development	**Customer** Over-Concentration Acquisition cost, time Retention
Scale System & process development Cost v revenue Hiring and retention, key-person risk Client and market development Logistics and infrastructure build Contract management	**People** Key-person risk Hiring, Training Retention Leadership capability Remuneration	**Supplier** Over-concentration Unfavourable terms Reliability Quality Logistics Internal capabilities
Stabilise Customer service/quality Productivity Revenue maximisation Staff retention, leadership Operational robustness – e.g. BCP, DR plans Business & system security IP protection Regulatory and legal compliance	**Process** Systems Capability Systems Scalability Data Privacy Cyber Security Client onboarding Customer service Quality Management BCP/DR plans	**Competitor** Pricing (price war) Reputation Poaching of staff
	Property Intellectual Property Premises Logistics infrastructure	**Constraints** Licensing Compliance Data, System Integrity
	Paperwork Compliance Contract Management Governance (Board, Management) Health & Safety ISO 9001	

Risk Management 101 — The Basics

There are entire forests of books about risk management. You may be glad to hear, this is not one of them! However, what I am going to do is summarise for you the basics of risk management in established businesses, and how they assess risk.

Understanding how larger businesses manage their risks is important to ensure you get your own business to scale. It will also help when you are discussing the risk profile of your business with owners, customers or other stakeholders.

You can build this profile by applying the following approach to the risks you've already identified in the section above. Some of this may seem rather clunky, but I have kept it to the absolute minimum. (I apologise in advance to any risk management specialists, who may wince at how much detail I have omitted!)

The Foundations of Risk Management

The basic principles of the risk management discipline can be seen in guidelines published by the ISO, which oversees standards on many aspects of business management. The risk management "family" of standards is what's known as ISO 31000.[32] This standard covers risk principles, assessment techniques, and the definitions used in risk management. There is a lot of detail. Good bedtime reading!

Specific risks are also covered in other ISO standards, aligned to the ISO 31000 guidelines. Business specialisms such as project management, information security, industrial processes, and financial portfolios all have their own specific risk management guidelines, which supplement the overall ISO 31000 framework.

In ISO 31000, "risk" is defined as "the possibility that an event will occur that adversely affects the achievement of an objective". The standard defines the ideal risk management process. This approach identifies risks,

---

32. See https://en.wikipedia.org/wiki/ISO_31000

impact and probability of occurring, and then confirms mitigation steps to reduce those risks (either probability or impact, or both).

Let's look next at what this means in practical terms.

Risk Management In Business

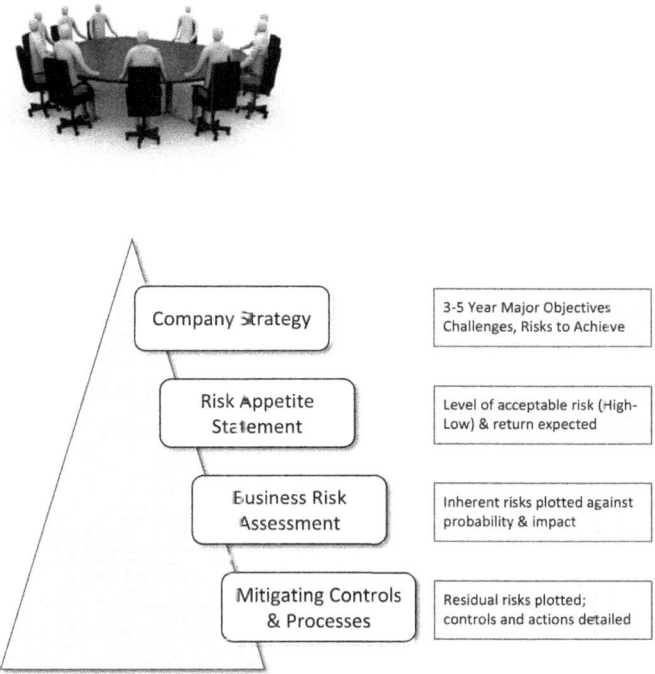

Figure 8.2: Risk Management Framework

Businesses that want to manage risk well adopt a top-down approach. This starts with a formal **company strategy,** which includes the major risks that may prevent the strategy being delivered. The risks identified are then translated into a **risk appetite statement**, which describes how much risk the business is prepared to accept (its "appetite" for risk). It should also indicate the cost needed to mitigate these risks, compared to the likely returns from the business strategy.

Some businesses do not bother with a risk appetite statement. But all of them would expect to complete a documented **business risk assessment**. This might vary a lot in level of detail provided, but at very least should rank and rate risks against a matrix of probability and expected impact, if it occurred. These risks would then be plotted on a "heat map" *(see Figure 8.3)*. Any risks in the high or extreme category must have mitigating plans in place to reduce their risk level as quickly as possible.

Probability		Impact				
		Very Low	Low	Medium	High	Very High
	Almost Certain	Medium	High	Extreme	Extreme	Extreme
	Likely	Medium	Medium	High	Extreme	Extreme
	Possible	Low	Medium	Medium	High	Extreme
	Unlikely	Low	Low	Medium	Medium	High
	Rare	Low	Low	Low	Medium	Medium

PROBABILITY	Occur < 12 months?	Event Without Mitigation
Almost Certain	100%	Has happened before in the business
Likely	50%	Will probably occur
Possible	10%	Has happened in other businesses
Unlikely	1%	Could occur, has rarely happened in business
Rare	0.10%	Exceptional, not seen before

IMPACT	Very Low	Low	Medium	High	Very High
Financial	Minimal	~ 1 week $ revenues	~1 month revenues	~ one quarter $ revenues	> 6 month $ revenues
Reputational Regulatory/Legal Operational/Technology People Strategic	Trivial: no noticed effect on objectives	Minor: may have undesirable outcomes	Major: challenge to achieve some objectives	Material: big impact and team distraction	Existential: big enough to put you out of business

Figure 8.3: Heat Map

Before they are mitigated, these risks are labelled "inherent" — that is, arising naturally from the business activity. Risk levels are assessed again after controls are put in place, and this is labelled "residual" risk.

RISK #	RISK TYPE	RISK DESCRIPTION	PROBABILITY (VH/H/M/L/VL)	IMPACT	INHERENT RISK RATING	MITIGATION/CONTROLS	PROBABILITY (VH/H/M/L/VL)	IMPACT	RESIDUAL RISK RATING	STATUS (of Mitigation)	TRAFFIC LIGHT STATUS**	RISK OWNER
1	TECHNOLOGY/Platform	Fail to develop/maintain IT platform to deliver expected capability to onboard/service customers	LIKELY	VERY HIGH	Extreme	1. Appoint CTO 2. External review of IT stack	POSSIBLE	HIGH	HIGH	1. CTO Appointed 1/9/20 2. External review underway, due 31/10	AMBER	CTO (once appointed)
2	FINANCE/Business Model	1. Fail to onboard customers at planned acquisition cost 2. Retention risk on customers	POSSIBLE	HIGH	High	1. Review CAC efficiency plans. 2. Launch channel partner campaign 3. Initiate customer service program	UNLIKELY	MEDIUM	LOW	1. CAC review complete. Proposals agreed. 2. Channel partner launch due 31/10 3. Service program onhold, new CMO reviewing	AMBER	CFO/CMO
3	FINANCE/Funding	1. Costs higher than expected 2. Funding exercise takes longer than expected to complete	LIKELY	HIGH	Extreme	1. Review costs against revenues weekly 2. Build contingency plan in cashflow forecast and bank facilities 3. Accelerate discussions with potential early stage investors	UNLIKELY	MEDIUM	MEDIUM	1. Ongoing 2. Complete. Bank facility agreed. 3. Underway, next meetings by 31/10	GREEN	CFO
4	PROCESS/Information Security	1. Exposure to cyber attack, ransomware 2. Loss of customer data/data piracy breaches	POSSIBLE	HIGH	High	1. End to end review of systems by external expert 2. Penetration testing of main systems by Trusted third party 3. Comms & training on phishing and other key risks to all staff	UNLIKELY	HIGH	MEDIUM	1. External expert appointed, review due 31/10 2. Pen testing complete 31/09 3. Training material drafted for onboarding + comms for staff 4. Regular phishing drill implemented i.e. third party tester	AMBER	CIU
5	PROCESS/Operational Disruption	1. Loss of building 2. Loss of core systems 3. Loss/unavailability of key staff (e.g. COVID19)	UNLIKELY	HIGH	Medium	1. BCP plans drawn up and tested 2. System DR plans built and tested; back up site built 3. Keyman risk identified and alternates/training/work-around plan identified	RARE	MEDIUM	LOW	1. BCP plan drafted, test planned for 30/11 2. DR plan drafted, cloud provider test due 15/10 3. 2 key roles identified; procedure mapping & knowledge transfer workshops planned by 30/11	GREEN	COO/CIO
6	COMPLIANCE/Failure to comply with legislation	1. Breach in HSE requirements in workplace 2. Failure to obtain required licenses 3. Failure to maintain all ATO/ASIC legal requirements	UNLIKELY	MEDIUM	Medium	1. Publish HSE Procedures, train staff, spot checks by management 2. Full review of required licenses with half yearly audit by external auditor 3. Annual walkthrough of compliance by accountant	RARE	LOW	LOW	1. Training included in staff induction; completion monitored and 100% complete 2. Last review completed 30/6 3. Review completed 30/6, 100% compliance	GREEN	COO/CFO
7	SUPPLIERS	Quality of product from supplier inconsistent	LIKELY	MEDIUM	High	1. Agree quality standards with suppliers & recourse if not acceptable 2. Establish QA team to review product on receipt 3. Check all customer feedback for any QA concerns, report back to supplier	RARE	LOW	LOW	1) QA expectations published to all suppliers - done 31/7 2. QA team leader hired, onboarding 1/11 3. Customer feedback Dashboard being built to capture all supplier-relevant feedback	AMBER	COO

** TRAFFIC LIGHT STATUS KEY: GREEN = On track, AMBER = Some Issues; RED = Off track

Figure 8.4: Risk Register Example

163

Businesses compile individual risk reduction plans into overall summaries of mitigating controls and processes, which are maintained as a **risk register**. Each risk should be detailed and actions specified to reduce its inherent rating *(see Figure 8.4 on previous page)*.

To complete the process, the residual risk is then plotted on the risk heat map, which provides a visual check that all major risks are well-managed *(see Figure 8.5)*.

Examples as per Risk Register items #1 and #5, from Figure 8.4.

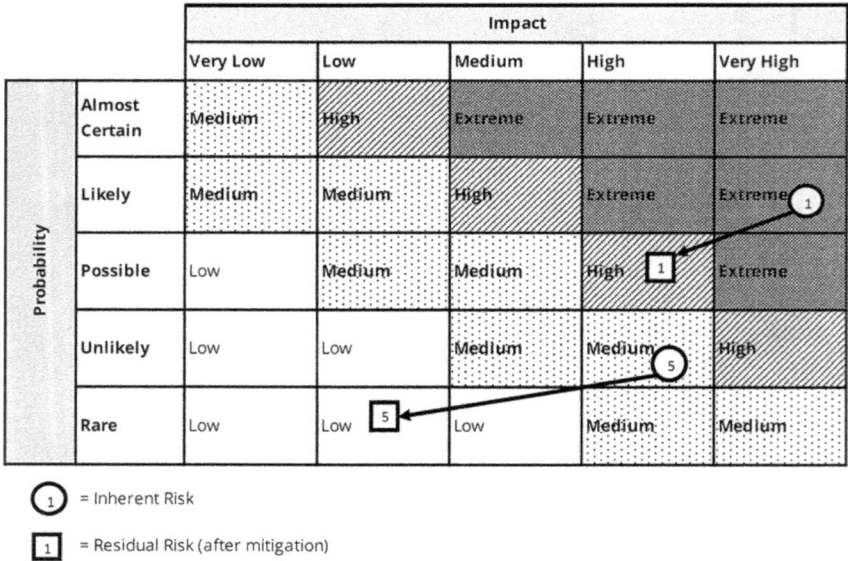

		Impact				
		Very Low	Low	Medium	High	Very High
Probability	Almost Certain	Medium	High	Extreme	Extreme	Extreme
	Likely	Medium	Medium	High	Extreme	Extreme ⓵
	Possible	Low	Medium	Medium	High [1]	Extreme
	Unlikely	Low	Low	Medium	Medium ⑤	High
	Rare	Low	Low [5]	Low	Medium	Medium

⓵ = Inherent Risk

[1] = Residual Risk (after mitigation)

Figure 8.5: Plotting Impact of Risk Mitigation

Despite spending a lot of time on risk management and mitigation during my career, I have heard little specific reference to ISO 31000. However, its principles and the elements described are widely used. The top-down summary of risks, the risk profile heat map and the risk assessment and mitigation plans are all features I've used in business and found useful (when kept brief).

You should note that the definitions of "impact" used (*as shown in Figure 8.3*) can and should be amended to make them as relevant as possible to your business. The key point here is to differentiate the really catastrophic risks from the simply irritating.

Using It in Your Business

If you are not familiar with it, this approach may seem like a lot of paperwork. It's true that in the wrong hands, it can be a tick-box exercise, which doesn't add much value. But if you use it well, it will help you focus on what needs doing and who should do it. I have used it myself in various roles (including scale-ups) and it has always helped identify things that I would not have thought about otherwise.

If you need help with facilitating this process, I recommend taking specialist advice. It will save you time and pain later on, when you really need it.

Don't forget that the value of going through this process is less about the documents that result from it, and more about the healthy discussion it provokes. So it's important to involve people who can challenge your thinking, not simply write down answers without query.

For those of you willing to give it a go, the following checklist gives the basic approach I recommend. You can also download a soft copy of the risk register template shown in Figure 8.4 at www. pellucid.global.

CHECKLIST: BUILDING YOUR RISK PROFILE

1. **Summarise your major risks** (as you identified in the "Risky You" section above) into the risk register. Group risks, if you can, for ease of management, based on either functional areas within your business (e.g. Technology, Operations, Finance), or the 5P framework provided in Chapter 3.

2. **Make a subjective assessment** on your current level of risk, or "inherent risk".

3. **Decide on mitigation actions for each major risk** — what's going to be done to remove or mitigate the risk. *You should list this in enough detail to be actioned by you or your team.*

4. **Assess post-mitigation risk level**: This is what's called "residual risk".

5. **Assign each risk and action to an owner**: Even in a one-person business, you will have other people involved — e.g. your accountant, whom you can list if it's a financial risk.

6. **Review your risks monthly**. Update the status of the risk, mitigating actions, and whether they are on track.

Risky Them — Stakeholders and Regulators

I've always thought it ironic that one big risk to running a scale-up is the way your key stakeholders perceive your risk management approach. The actual act of not managing risk well is also a risk! If they think your approach is a problem, these stakeholders can slow you down, or even shut you down.

Why Would They Have a Problem?

Your stakeholders know you have a greater appetite for risk than they do. That's why you're the leader of the scale-up, not them. There's an asymmetry of risk and reward for stakeholders and regulators, as opposed to you. If you take risks and succeed, you will reap big rewards. However, regulators (and some board members) will not receive any extra reward if you scale up but may be in trouble if you introduce a lot more risk into the market in which you are active.

So stakeholders will want to be sure you understand risk, you know how to manage it, and that you have credible plans to do so.

How you talk about risk, and whether you talk the same language as the stakeholder, can also be important in building their confidence in you. Regulators have a specific focus on how you manage your major risks, and usually have formidable powers to ensure you pay attention to their views.

What Could Possibly Go Wrong?

It takes many good deeds to build a good reputation, and only one bad one to lose it. So said the famous entrepreneur and US Founding Father, Benjamin Franklin.

Investors, regulators and stakeholders — who can be major customers or partners — know that things can often go wrong. Usually these are things that no one expected at the outset. Nassim Taleb's famous 2007 book *The Black Swan*[33] highlights the impact of rare and unpredictable outlier events. Although "black swan" risks are highly unlikely, stakeholders will expect you to show you have considered them and put in place potential mitigation steps, if they consider it appropriate.

If you're not thinking about potential risks, bad outcomes can multiply. Even big businesses have failed to manage risks well in the eyes of the regulator, and then made it worse by trying to hide the fact.

Several classic "brush it under the carpet" moments were visible in the recent Hayne Royal Commission into Misconduct in the Australian Banking, Superannuation and Financial Services Industry. The venerable fund manager AMP was heavily criticised when the Commission reviewed its processes. AMP had an external report on its risk

---

33. *The Black Swan: The Impact of the Highly Improbable,* Nassim Taleb, Random House, 2007.

management processes prepared for its regulator (APRA), but the AMP board edited out the parts critical of the company. This misconduct led to the forced departure of the CEO, the chair and much of the board, as well as the loss of billions of dollars in market value.

There are other cases of scale-ups falling foul of regulatory or legal issues, which better risk management may well have prevented. Some examples are:[34]

- In the mid-2000s, the MP3 streaming business **Zor** was shut down while still competitive because it infringed on intellectual property.
- **Guvera,** Gold Coast, Australia, was also running a streaming business on a much bigger scale. It raised $180 million in 2008, intending to compete with Spotify. Having bought a business called Blinkbox in 2015, it failed to honour the entitlements of its employees, who then sued it successfully for $3 million. It also had investors complaining to ASIC, which led to it being blocked on the Australian Stock Exchange (ASX).
- **CanadaDrugs.com**[35] provided mail-order medications, and misled USA customers that they had US FDA[36] approval when they didn't. The FDA accused them of illegally importing and selling branded and unapproved drugs and shut them down in December 2017.

Your major stakeholders will want to know that your scale-up:

- understands its risks — including those specific to the scale-up — so you can describe them in simple, jargon-free terms;
- has a process to review and mitigate the risks;
- can show actions taken and progress, as needed.

---

34. Source: "What Went Wrong?" https://www.lessonsatstartup.com/2020/01/09/list-of-famous-failed-australian-startups-and-businesses/
35. https://www.canadadrugsonline.com/CanadaDrugsCom.aspx
36. Food and Drug Administration.

It's possible that you or your leadership team might feel this doesn't apply to them. Perhaps you think you are not in a risky business and not in a regulated industry, so this is all theoretical. Unfortunately for you, in almost every country and industry, there will be a regulator that cares about what you're doing! Stakeholders will not always insist on a formal risk review, but they do expect you to be well-managed, and the risk review process is an important part of that.

So, with that in mind, let's finish our risk review with a quick checklist of actions to keep your business out of trouble with the stakeholders and regulators.

CHECKLIST: STAKEHOLDER RISK MANAGEMENT

- **Consider the regulators in your industry and research their expectations and regulations**. If you need it, get legal or specialist help to do this. The effort and expense will be worth it.

- If you're selling directly to customers and consumers, **ensure you understand the Australian Consumer Law (ACL) protections**. The Australian Competition and Consumer Commission (ACCC) website[37] is worth checking out to get some basic guidance.

- **Review potential competitors** for IP, trademark or branding issues. Don't get caught out by the obvious.

The Good News

Many scale-up leaders may find this whole topic out of their comfort zone. It will feel alien and very specialist, and some leaders may not want to share their risk template with anyone outside their immediate team.

---

37. https://www.accc.gov.au/consumers/consumer-rights-guarantees

Remember that most stakeholders welcome seeing a proactive discussion about risks in the business. They see it as a sign of good management. You don't need to publish your specific risk register but sharing your assessment of risks with stakeholders will help to flush out anything that may concern them, including issues they may not understand well.

Conclusion

Scale-up leaders that manage risk well understand that it is one of the keys to success, even if it is not always the most exciting or natural management task. Documenting risk is a critical first step to managing it, and your stakeholders and regulators will appreciate it.

Don't delegate this activity to specialists, consultants or staff members. It's tempting, but don't do it. If you (the business leader) consider your major risks and can discuss them with confidence, that's 80% of the value of the risk management process.

One other problem — documenting every little thing — should also be avoided. It can occur if people confuse risks (what might happen) with issues (what's already happening). Most issues do need management but there's no point mitigating them. They need management now. You need to think about risk as a future potential issue that needs a plan. If you have over 10 risks listed, it means you are either too detailed, or you have a risk management plan unlikely to be delivered!

Next Steps

Managing risk well is something all mature enterprises need to do. If you've followed the Scale without Fail approach on your scale-up journey, you'll have built an enterprise that will need to be managed differently from when it was in fast-growth mode. Our last chapter looks at how you should manage a larger business for continued success, now you've reached the Stabilise stage of your S-curve growth.

CHAPTER 9
Stabilise – Managing Your Business at Scale

Finally your business has reached the end of your original growth forecast, and the rate of change has naturally slowed. You're not the same business anymore, so what kind of business are you? How will you manage? What will your priorities be to ensure you continue to succeed in this new world? You might see this as a good problem: "We'll work out our end state when we get through the scale up!" But it's best to set a clear goal and build things once, not to rebuild them later.

Otherwise, a number of undesirable things might happen. First, the **change to business as usual** could be a bigger change or management shock than expected, which could distract and even damage business performance. Second, it could be **harder to hire and motivate people**. They may not understand what their role is going to be in the future. Third, it could be **harder to build capability**—it is *easier to build capability while in the scale-up phase.* For example, you can design the business for efficiency — looking at the location of staff, the level of automation, the level of outsourcing etc.

You'll also find that the **culture you want is easier to embed in your business** when built during the change period, rather than afterwards. Business managers that go through a lot of change reach the same conclusion. They realise that the difference between the normal or BAU state of a business, and the change state, is huge.

In the BAU state, you will literally run your business as usual, and everything will generally be stable and static while you're doing business. But during periods of major change, you will be moving a lot of things around. If you try to mix those two states, your business becomes very difficult to manage. This is like trying to move furniture around at the same time as sitting on it. Not an easy thing to do!

Define Your Target Business

The good news is the large amount of help available to define how your "mature" business should be organised and run. Let's look at the theory first, before we dive into some practical specifics for your business.

The modern theory behind how you should organise and run a large business goes back to the end of World War II. In 1943, Peter Drucker was invited in to study the management practices of General Motors (now GM). It was then one of the largest companies in the world, and run by long-time CEO Alfred P. Sloan, whose management innovations in GM were credited with having transformed the way that cars were built. Based on his observations within GM, Drucker published a book in 1946 called *Concept of the Corporation*, which was widely seen as the first of its kind to describe how a large organisation worked.

Drucker's focus was on people, and how management made a business tick. Alfred Sloan was an engineer who was focused on policies, systems, and structures. The debate between those two viewpoints continues today, although it seems likely Sloan's views prevailed within GM. Unfortunately, that didn't turn out well for GM, because over time it faded into a shadow of its former glory. After 100 years in business, it fell into bankruptcy and was then rescued in 2008: 21,000 workers were fired, 20 factories and 400 dealers were closed. Ten years later, at the time of writing, it remains one of the largest car makers in the world, but its market capitalisation of $37 billion is dwarfed by Tesla at $151 billion. It's fallen a long way from being one of the most valuable businesses in the world.

Modern analysts consider that the right kind of business is neither all Drucker nor all Sloan, out both. You need to combine both people <u>and</u> processes to build a successful and sustainable company. Both aspects are important when you're designing your target business for the future.

More recently, Jim Collins and Jerry Porras wrote a famous business book called *Built to Last*.[38] They studied 18 "visionary" companies that remained successful over a long period, and boiled success down to three things unique to those companies:

- They **outlived their initial leaders** and exceeded the business scope set by them.
- They **adopted a continuous-improvement mindset** — a culture of trying a lot of things to see what worked and discarding the rest.
- They **were vision-based**, which meant that they always set themselves stretching targets — what Collins called "big, hairy, audacious goals (BHAGs)" — and an almost cult-like culture around focusing on more than just profits.

As a scale-up leader, your focus is on dealing with huge growth right now, rather than spending time thinking about the long-term future of your business. That's to be expected. However, many businesses get to the top of their S-curve not knowing "what good looks like" as they exit their growth stage. Unless you have worked in large organisations as well as small ones, it can be hard to spot what is needed for your business to succeed over time. As we've seen with General Motors, just getting to scale is not a guarantee of surviving or thriving in the long term.

The Key Elements of Your Mature Business

As we said earlier in this book, it's a good idea to "begin with the end in mind".[39] You need to paint the picture of your own destination, which will be unique to you and your business. In this chapter, my

---

38. *Built to Last: Successful Habits of Visionary Companies*, Harper Business, 1994.
39. Habit #2 of *"Seven Habits of Highly Effective People"*, Stephen Covey, 1989.

aim is to give you some ideas to help you to do that. These will be practical ideas, drawn from my 30 years' business experience, my work with other scale-ups, and the most relevant ideas from the best management theorists.

Every scale-up leader needs to consider a number of key themes and operating principles for their mature organisation. I use the term "steady state" to denote this mature business, as fast growth slows down and the organisation settles into a different rhythm.

These themes are grouped into the five topics we will step through in this chapter. They are:

1. Transition from hyper-growth to the Stabilise stage
2. Key elements of the steady-state business
3. Steady-state operating principles
4. Steady-state personal leadership habits
5. What next: Raising the bar on "change as usual".

"Are We There Yet?": From Hyper-Growth to the Stabilise Stage

Like the Starship Enterprise dropping out of warp speed, the business universe at your destination will seem very different from the one it was when you started your growth journey. The first question for you as the business leader to tackle is: What is your arrival point? Can you describe it simply to yourself and anyone else? Learning to signal this clearly will also help you get your team to the end goal successfully. You can draw on the Compass, SOAP and ScaleCast work to help you describe this clearly.

Arrival Point

To set an arrival point is important for everyone — not just for yourself as the leader, but also for the team. You need something to aim for, and to pace yourselves. To mark when your current way of working is going to settle down. This is also sending signals to the team and your stakeholders that you are a thoughtful leader — one who foreshadows events, not just reacts to them.

Of course, every scale-up leader will be keen not to appear to be declaring success too early. None of us would want the George Bush experience, where the US President stood on an aircraft carrier in 2003 and declared "Mission Accomplished!" during the Iraq War. Sadly, the war intensified and went on to a more horrible stage. We don't want that.

However, the benefits of setting and hitting a clear target outweigh the risk of calling success too early. It's better to aim high and fall short than to have no target at all.

Transition

Signalling and properly managing the transition to steady state will help settle the team into the new state quickly and calmly. If you don't refocus on new targets in your now-larger business, you will risk remaining in a fast-growth frenzy, which can lead to burnout and distraction. In the "fight or flight" mode of your peak-growth period, you will not be able to remain productive for the long-term.

I used to do a lot of rowing. In a rowing race, you start very fast at the highest rate of strokes per minute the crew can manage. This gets the boat going but is unsustainable after the first minute. You can't keep going at that pace; you are sprinting and burning up an enormous amount of energy and oxygen.

After that first burst, good crews lengthen their stroke, slow the stroke rhythm down, and focus on making their strokes longer, stronger and smoother. This way the whole crew settles into a longer, sustainable rhythm, one that they can continue for the duration of the race. They've always got the option to put in a faster burst if the race demands, much like a business can handle periods of extra effort once it reaches steady state. But without shifting to a different cadence or rhythm, the crew cannot keep going as they did when they first started.

After leading numerous major change initiatives throughout my career, I found that the team I'm leading has always wanted to know when the current sprint is going to slow down, and what their world will be like when we get to the arrival point.

Despite this transition, you and your team will still expect your business to continue to grow and improve after this point. How you manage this change of gear is also a clear symbol of the kind of business you want to manage in the future.

The Theory of Change

Change management has been studied by analysts for a long time. An organisational psychologist called Kurt Lewin[40] proposed in the early 20th century that businesses go through three stages during change.

He described these stages as **freeze, unfreeze,** and **refreeze**, with change happening during the "unfreeze" phase and the organisation moving to a new "steady state" after that change was over. Lewin highlighted that after a change was complete, it is important to bring stability back to the business. Leaders needed to focus people on the new expected behaviours and performance levels. If this doesn't happen, then normal human behaviour is to slide back into prior habits, which is not usually effective in the new state of the organisation.

So both practice and theory confirm that good management of this transition from growth to steady state is important to the future success of the business.

---

40. Kurt Lewin, "Frontiers in Group Dynamics: Concept, Method and Reality in Social Science; Social Equilibria and Social Change", *Human Relations*, June 1947.

CHECKLIST: ARRIVAL & TRANSITION

- Set out a clear arrival target for your business — time, turnover, geographic coverage. I suggest a maximum of two years from the start of the scale-up.

- Communicate progress towards that target along the way through email updates, morning teas, "town hall" updates and presentations to the team.

- Celebrate arrival with suitable presentations — office open days for stakeholders, team members, etc.

- Make symbolic changes to how you manage or communicate, including team appointments and other positions, and also reset the expected performance targets.

Steady State: Key Elements of Your Business

Until now, you may have got by with everyone doing a bit extra when needed, to cover the gaps where no-one had official responsibility for that task or function. Now you've got to put in place the functions that larger, stable businesses need for the longer term. What's important, and what's not, depends on the kind of business you're in, and the scale that you built. For example, an international multi-market software business is very different from a national product sales business. However, all businesses need some basic things to be done well, and these are the key elements you should consider.

What Good Looks Like

Unless you've worked in a larger business, you may be uncertain how a functioning one looks like. Many of your staff may not either. Even if you do come from a bigger business, your experience may not include how to set up the different functions that you need to run a larger company.

The unfortunate fact is that problem areas (and staff) will take up 80% of your time. This is true even when they're individuals who are not critical to delivering your formal strategy. For example, if you have a team leader who does not work out, this can demoralise the whole team and damage productivity.

Understanding whether your team member can deliver the required standard of work in the steady-state business is important. So is having complete clarity about what each function (e.g. Sales, Marketing, Communications) is supposed to do, to avoid confusion and overlap between each function. Unclear responsibilities will always lead to disputes and sub-optimal performance in those functions.

Even when you're not an expert in each functional area, you must have worked through your overall view of the business when you get to your arrival point. You will then be more ready to lead and structure the business when you're at scale. You should seek help when you need it, but the more forethought you can bring to this work, the better your outcomes and the smaller your problems are likely to be.

What Are the Key Functions?

A vast amount of material exists on how businesses should best manage themselves, under the topic "organisational development" or OD. In summary, every business legally has to be able to do a certain minimum number of things. You need to be able to manage your finances, sales, people, suppliers, IT and legal commitments.

You can organise how you do these things (and other functions) in a number of different ways, depending on your personal preference and the type of business you are in. For example, if you're great at sales or business development, you might decide you can provide that function, alongside your role as leader or CEO. Or you might be a tech wiz, so you decide you can also be the chief IT officer — like Bill Gates, when Microsoft first started. You can even outsource many of your functions if you choose, in which case you may want to revisit the "Core v context" discussion we covered in the Strategy Compass work in Chapter 2.

A lot of new businesses prefer to keep their organisations fluid and non-bureaucratic. And I would too. But even big businesses that "go agile" ensure that they establish clear functional accountability. If you don't think about these points early enough, you may end up having to put **unplanned people hires** into your budget (and costs too), when you could have avoided this with some forward planning.

We can take a lead here from how venture capitalists assess your business. They will always ask who is in the business leadership, because they want to reduce key-person risk (i.e. over-dependence on a few key people who may not stay). They want to be sure that you're gaining functional expertise and that you're increasing your leadership capacity to handle your business as it gets larger.

It's easy to focus on areas that you like or understand well. But you need to set up a complete business and appoint functional leads that can cover your blind spots, even though you personally don't need to master every single function in detail. However, to make this a little easier on you, I've provided a simplified memory jogger for the major functions I would expect to see in most businesses. (*See Table 9.1.*)

CHECKLIST: DEFINING KEY ELEMENTS OF YOUR BUSINESS

- **Identify your major functional needs**: Review your business against the "Key Business Functions" checklist.

- **Decide how you should be organised**: Do you need geographical or market leads, or both? Do you need extra management layers, given the size or spread of the business? *Try to avoid having more than 10 people reporting to one manager* (i.e. add extra team leaders), unless the role is very simple.

- **Decide whether you can outsource functions**: Do you really need to run a customer service team? Can you contract out IT development, HR or marketing?

- **Size the functions in approximate terms**: How many people do you need to manage that responsibility? *Consider backup or deputies to cover when key people are sick or busy elsewhere.*

- **Review your current team against your needs**: Do this only when you've got the target structure worked out, so you *don't twist your business to fit your current resources.* I've seen this happen too many times, and it never ends well. Don't design the organisation for the people you have; design your structure for the things that need to be done. Otherwise you risk limiting the performance of your business.

- **Consider transitional roles for your current team**: You want to retain intellectual property or knowledge in your team while you continue to build the company for the future. If your current team members are not right as the future functional leaders, you may want them in training or other development roles, to help translate the business into its new steady-state structure.

- **Check all roles have clear accountability**: New people in new jobs take time to work out their priorities. Clear job descriptions with minimal overlap of responsibilities with other roles will minimise confusion and unproductive "turf battles" between managers.

Table 9.1: Key Business Functions

Domain	Business Function
Customer/ Market Facing	• Business Development (can include BD Strategy) • Sales & Marketing (can be separate) • Customer Service (if in Sales role: can be in Operations)
Execution	• Operations • Continuous Improvement (or: Ops or Change Mgt) • IT (can be split between Development and BAU: "IT Ops") • Customer Service • Change/Project Management (extra to IT-only projects)
Enablers	• Finance (budgets, payroll, AP/AR, banking, corp accounts) • Management Reporting/Analytics (can be part of Finance) • HR (can include Learning & Development) • Communications (internal, PR, social media) • Office Management (can be part of other functions) • Strategy • Company Secretarial (can be part of Legal)
Control	• Legal • Compliance/Internal Audit (or part of Legal or Risk) • Risk (includes BCP Planning, in FSI: also Credit risk) • Security (can be part of IT for IS Security) • Quality Control (can be aligned with Ops) • Health & Safety (HSE)
Supplier Management	• Third Party/ Vendor Management/Procurement • Property Management
Market-Facing Options	• Geographic Heads (e.g. state, country, regional leads) • Product/Offering leads (if distinct disciplines, e.g. different consulting topics – Risk, Strategy, IT, etc.) • Market Verticals (e.g. finance, health)

Keep It Simple

There's a lot to consider in designing your future organisation. Don't expect it to be perfect but be prepared to iterate. Work on the basis that maintaining steady state is a different task from scaling up, and therefore a different organisation is needed. You will need to make major changes, even though you may be unsure about all of your moves. You will find — as I have done — that every business is different, and no organisational model is perfect, however hard you work at it. You should aim to build the best organisation you can, and where you need to leave areas undefined, try to make these in areas you know well, or feel well-equipped to handle.

One final point: organisations often budget less money than needed to develop the business. Specialist capabilities are needed to improve your business when at scale, such as **new business development, process improvement, performance management**, and **IT enhancement**. Your steady-state business plan needs to include them, or risk being unable to evolve to meet future stakeholder expectations. If your budget has the room, these capabilities are always worth the money.

Steady State: Operating Principles

You've managed your team from the early Start pilot stage all the way through the scale-up frenzy. You've all grown and learned a lot along the way. Now it's time to think about doing things differently.

We've talked about transitioning the team and setting out the functions for the scaled-up business. We also need to look at changing the way things run on a daily basis. Our goal now is to move from the attitude of "whatever it takes" to a more <u>sustainable</u> way of managing ourselves and the business.

The operating model for your steady-state business has to be easy to understand and self-sustaining. When they join, new staff expect things to work, from induction training to setting business goals, and other day-to-day operating processes. When you bring in new people

STABILISE — MANAGING YOUR BUSINESS AT SCALE

after you've had a tight-knit team working on a scale-up, getting them up to speed quickly and making everyone feel included is critical. This is where adopting broader operating principles can help.

Built for Success

Good businesses help everyone achieve more with less effort, because they have built processes and disciplines to make it harder for good people to make mistakes. They don't rely on great people doing the exceptional every day, just to deliver the plan.

I remember my first time in a start-up. Everyone did everything. The whole team turned up to debate the website and the customer proposition, like little boys following the football around the pitch. We all focused on the same topic. In a scale-up, everyone is pitching-in and doing what it takes to get the minimum viable product working at scale. When you're in a team of 20 or fewer, you remember everyone's name, background, strengths and weaknesses. Once you get to a team of more than 50 people, you'll be struggling to keep names, backgrounds and skills straight.

As your business gets larger, you have to put systems and processes in place to run it effectively. You can't rely on daily contact and discussion like you did when you were a smaller team. It's especially true if some of your team are based in another location, as knowing how to manage people remotely is a distinct management skill. Once you have established these new ways of working, you will find it easier to implement the continuous improvement discipline that Collins and Porras tells us[41] is one of the key traits of great companies.

41. *Built to Last: Successful Habits of Visionary Companies.*

So it's not just about the operational processes being improved, but also how the company organises and runs itself.

How Much Detail?

You might end up feeling that defining your operating principles is simply bureaucracy, and low priority. You'll get around to it when you have spare time (i.e. never), or delegate the details to HR, or someone else on the team.

Just remember this is your best chance to get the business working at scale the way you want it to. It's not a one-off process, and it needs continued input from the person who owns it — that's you, the leader. You can delegate the crafting of the details, but you cannot delegate the principles. "What gets checked, gets done"[42] is something I've observed play out in every job and business. If you (or your nominated delegate) is not following up on these points regularly, don't be surprised if they fail to stick. Iterate and follow up, as always.

Let's run through some major operating principles every steady-state business should be able to demonstrate.

---

42. My version of the saying attributed to Peter Drucker: "What gets measured, gets managed".

CHECKLIST: KEY OPERATING PRINCIPLES

- Ensure everyone has **clear job descriptions** and check there are no unintentional responsibility overlaps. Check that the job descriptions from roles that existed in the scale-up stage are still accurate in the new organisation.

- Set out **KPIs** for everyone on the team, based on the company goals. Your KPIs as a leader should cascade directly to your team and then on down to every employee, so they can see how what they do contributes to the overall success of the company.

- Develop a simple **MIS** and **performance dashboards** around those KPIs. Cascade them down to every single person in the team, if possible.[43]

- Build a simple **operating rhythm** — a combination of operational daily huddles led by team leads, weekly management meetings, monthly informal reviews, and quarterly board stakeholder reviews.

- Develop **internal communications**. This should include regular (weekly or monthly) morning-tea briefings, stand-up presentations and informal newsletters. *Don't assume everyone knows all the important stuff*, nor that they'll naturally get on with each other, unless you encourage them to.

Is That Everything?

As you'll understand if you've run a larger business, this is not a detailed playlist on everything you'll need to run the place successfully. However, applying the 80/20 Rule, these principles are the ones that

---

43. You might <u>not</u> cascade metrics that you consider commercially sensitive, such as $ or % profit margins.

should apply to every post scale-up business. They need time and effort invested from you and your team to get going, particularly the SOAPs, management information dashboards, and induction programs. But they pay back quickly and keep on doing so after the scale-up is complete.

Steady State: Personal Leadership Habits

Once you have set up the <u>who</u> and <u>what</u> of your organisation, now you should consider the <u>how</u>. And how your business runs will be shaped by how <u>you</u> run it.

One of the key factors in every business is what's called "tone from the top". This is a combination of messages and behaviours of the leadership of the business. Across many years of working in and for businesses, I've seen the importance of this when a change of leader and approach has either revitalised the team or destroyed it. If the leadership team shows a lack of interest or experience in the steady-state operation, this may cause problems, magnified across a business team that's now larger.

For you, this means thinking about what you <u>do</u> and what you <u>say</u>, and whether your leadership style needs to change as your business transitions from scale-up to steady state.

More Than Words

Human communication experts tell us[44] that *it's not what you say, but how you say it*. Words account for 7% of communication, tone of voice accounts for 38%, and body language accounts for 55%. How you speak and act is more important than what you say. Also important is the congruence between words and actions. We instinctively pay most attention when we see an inconsistency between what someone says and what they do.

---

44. Professor Albert Mehrabian: *Silent messages: Implicit communication of emotions and attitudes,* Wadsworth, 1980.

This is why it is so important to change your style of management as your business transitions from being a smaller, high-growth business to a larger, more mature one. In the insurance claim repair scale-up I ran, I told my team leaders that I would manage them differently when we were at scale, and I did. Our focus in the scale-up phase was on rapidly getting resources onboard and trained to handle the accelerating work volumes. In the steady-state phase, we had much more focus on KPI metrics, BAU compliance, team engagement, communications, and team leadership. We had these functions during the scale-up phase but put much less focus on them.

You may have to manage your own preferred management style when you're making a transition like this. You may prefer to lead by example in building the nuts and bolts solutions in the business growth stages, but now the business needs you to provide more strategic direction, and a visible inspiring presence for the larger team. You will have to change from being fast-paced and outcome-focused, to a calmer and more detail-focused leadership style.

I Like Myself As I Am

You may find that you and even some of your staff think, "I'm not going to change who I am simply because the business is bigger". Your past success during the earlier stages of the business, or even running other businesses before this one, may have convinced you that you don't need to change your management approach, even if the business is different.

If you really don't need to change your approach between scale-up and steady state to get the most out of your business, I would say that is rare. I suggest that you get external input on this, including stakeholder input and employee surveys, to check that your management approach is what the business needs.

I'm not suggesting a personality transplant! But in a bigger business, people will have less individual time with you than before. You need to be mindful of the impact of this change on your leadership approach. If you are not comfortable, *consider whether you're the right person to lead the company through this next phase.* If you decide not, that wouldn't be unusual in a scale-up business and calling it out proactively is a sign of strength, not weakness.

Getting Help

The decisions you make set precedents. Don't allow behaviours if you don't want them repeated. You need to set boundaries and put formal disciplinary processes in place. This is particularly important in bigger businesses. A small business may accept behaviour that won't work in a larger business. For example, someone who is slack at turning up to meetings, or is sloppy at finishing tasks, will struggle to fit in with a larger business. Expectations will change around how people treat each other too. People who don't know each other well need to be more careful that their communication is considered appropriate at all times.

Personal behavioural issues like this can be confronting and difficult to address. Getting professional coaching on how to manage these issues may be a worthwhile investment, both for you as a leader and for your senior team.

CHECKLIST: PERSONAL LEADERSHIP IN STEADY STATE

- Decide on your **key personal messages** and what you expect from your team. Aim for consistency, clarity, simplicity.

- Remember that you **role model** the relationship you expect from the team. If you want confident, planned and calm behaviours, then plan your communications and meetings accordingly.

- Get **feedback from staff** through surveys and informal one-to-one or "skip levelling" — that is, talking directly to the direct reports of your individual reports.

- Focus on **managing by exception**. In a bigger business, you cannot manage everything. If you micromanage, you may stifle your team. By all means check details on occasion but set clear outcomes you expect and then delegate responsibility for delivery to others.

- **Differentiate between the formal and informal.** Some meetings should be "meetings of record" where you review performance, and track progress formally — for example, risk, personal development, strategy, IT and project development. You need to hold people accountable for outcomes, not details, and then follow up.

- **Communicate expected behaviours**, reward good examples, and punish poor behaviour.

It's Hard To Be Hard

One of the hard things about being a manager is when you have staff members with behaviour or performance issues. Sometimes they may be in denial about the impact of their behaviour, or they may not realise that they are underperforming. However tough it is, you should deal with the issue as quickly and cleanly as you can, as such problems rarely get better without any intervention and are highly likely to get worse. Don't tolerate what's wrong; no one will thank you for that.

They _will_ thank you for leading them with personal energy and competence, aligned to consistent and simple management disciplines. All of which increase the day-to-day certainty of how things get done for everyone in the business.

Steady State Plus: Raising the Bar on "Change as Usual"

It's tempting to sit back after a hectic change period and enjoy the slower pace after the scale-up growth eases. But business does not sit still, and neither can you. Once you build your "at scale" steady-state operation, you need to ensure it's also able to deliver steady and continuous improvement and performance.

More To Do

It's unlikely you'll hit every goal in your scale-up period. Some follow-up work has to be left until later when you have more time and more capability in the business. You'll also need to keep an eye on your competitors, who will start to react, as you are now a major player in their industry.

Apart from these obvious opportunities and threats, continued growth also helps with strengthening and upgrading the business, even in steady state. It's much easier to hire and retain good people if they can see you're still going somewhere, that you've got an engaging strategic vision — which in turn creates further opportunities for staff development.

In my experience, stakeholders will also expect more from the business than "just" business as usual.

Another S-Curve?

Harvard professor Clayton Christensen studied[45] the progress of many innovative technology firms in the 1990s. He found that they had to reinvent themselves constantly, to remain successful in their industries, and he called this reinvention "disruptive innovation". They needed to go up new S-curves once they'd reached the top of the last one, or be displaced by a more agile, fast-growing competitor.

Not all businesses are in markets as mercilessly competitive as the technology industries studied by Christensen. The general messages from his work, however, do apply to almost all businesses, especially in markets where a scale-up is possible (as you will have just proven!).

---

45. Clayton M. Christensen, *The Innovator's Dilemma: When New Technologies Cause Great Firms to Fail*, 1997.

You will need constantly to raise your performance to avoid being outcompeted, and as a disruptive new entrant you can expect to attract a reaction from your competitors as you get to a substantial size.

However, if you develop a culture that expects and delivers continuous improvement, this will help you perform better in a competitive situation. You will:

- attract and retain better staff
- deliver better products and customer service
- extract better margins — either through lower costs or higher quality or higher priced products.

All of these benefits support the need to build an expectation of CAU rather than BAU in your steady-state organisation. As well as bigger change projects, you should look for constant smaller improvements in how things are done in the business. This will keep alive the culture of agility that will have been dominant in your scale-up phase, even as you settle into a more stable operational rhythm.

CHECKLIST: EMBEDDING CAU

- **Embed continuous improvement disciplines** — such as *agile, lean operations or Six Sigma quality*[46] — **in your business with senior leadership accountability**: This may require specialised resources. If so, ensure they are held to clear outcomes with measurable ROI (return on investment).

- **Develop and communicate a CAU culture**: Engage all of your staff through idea schemes and incentives for improvement ideas. Celebrate your successes. (These were very successful in many of the large operations I ran.)

---

46. **Agile** usually refers to a method for building technology faster than more traditional approaches. **Lean operations** addresses waste and inefficiency in production, service and other process activities. **Six Sigma** is a quality method that seeks to minimise errors and quality variations in outputs of all kinds.

- **Benchmark your business against the best** (not just your immediate competitors): Set your frame of reference high, and check progress against your benchmarks regularly.

- **Invest management time and attention**: Your future-focused discussions should not be about just strategy or budgets, but also about how to improve the way the business works and what it delivers. Appoint members of your senior leadership as **champions** of specific cross-business improvement initiatives.

A mixed BAU and CAU environment may be unfamiliar to you and your team. However, you will be able to find plenty of good specialist advice on these themes, so don't hesitate to seek external support as needed to set you on the right track. Because CAU should deliver your business a positive ROI (including paying for any staff or other costs needed to deliver the improvements) the downsides should be limited. You should also see a great opportunity to develop and train your staff and future leaders, as well as improve your current business.

Conclusion

If you have a clear idea of where you're going, you are more likely to get to your goal, when and how you want. Plan well ahead for how the business will run and how you will manage it, and you will be more likely to succeed <u>after</u> the scale-up, not just during the growth period.

A lot of specific decisions need to be taken. People-based and personal behaviours are always hard topics to deal with effectively in any business. As we've discussed, *you can't expect change without changing yourself.* This is a key part of building sustainable success. But I am confident that if you take onboard the actions in the checklists above, adjusted as needed for your specific situation, you will see continued success.

Where Next?

We've reached "the end of the beginning" of your business success. You've completed climbing your first S-curve of growth and built a sustainable business. It's a business that is set to continue improving and is ready to move on to your next S-Curve!

Conclusion

Scale-up is exciting, scary and risky. If it's done well, it's also hugely rewarding. It creates value for many more people than the founding team and their investors.

Every scale-up is different but one thing is always the same. Whether it's new customers, new people, or new ways of doing things — everything comes at you *fast*, and you have little time to think and decide. The types of *challenges* scale-ups face are similar: people, finance, stakeholders Under pressure you need to do more than simply "wing it", and risk falling on your face.

Even if you are by experience and preference a "seat of the pants" type of businessperson, scaling-up means you must become, at least in part, a planner. If you don't do that, your risk of failure goes up dramatically.

It's important to know what you're aiming at: your big goal. But that's not enough. The bigger your scale-up goal, the more detail you need, preferably captured in a plan on paper, which you can iterate and improve as you go. With iteration, planning becomes learning, and learning improves your planning.

Of course, you don't need to plan every last detail before you begin. You can use the 80/20 Rule just as I have in this book. I've told you the 20% you <u>must</u> know to succeed and left the remaining 80% for you to discover as you build your business.

Let's remember why you're doing this scale-up in the first place: *to build a business very different from the one it is today.* A business built to last, one that is valuable and unique, which will change your life for the better, as well as the lives of many others. Along the way, there will be pressure, distractions and mishaps. But when you follow the steps I've outlined, I know you'll be able to build a scaled-up business, because you've planned how to avoid or manage pitfalls ahead of time.

Even the richest man in the world recognised that results can take longer to come than most expect. *All overnight success takes about 10 years,* said Jeff Bezos. And a large part of this time is spent getting the sequence of events right and planning ahead.

Having a plan does not mean your business is less fun or less flexible. In fact, the opposite is true. Knowing you have a recipe for success means you can focus your energy on the things that are unique to you and your scale-up. Get this right and you'll be in a minority of scale-up leaders who get where they intend to go. If you build a solid plan, it won't take 10 years to know you're on the right track.

The Scale without Fail Approach

Now you've read the book, you will be ready to scale up your business. You will:

- Define your end goal in enough detail that you can see when you are not going the right way, using the Strategy Compass and the SOAP framework.
- Frame the effort needed and the reward expected, through shirt sizing your plan.
- Build a timeline for your plan to scale up, based on your explicit assumptions, and capture this in your ScaleCast.
- Consider and document your approach to key elements in scaling the S-curve, including finance, people and stakeholders.
- Review and mitigate your key execution risks.
- Finally, define your arrival point. Describe what your business looks like at scale and how you will manage it, with your team and key stakeholders

If you want a quick reminder of what we've covered, have a look at the infographic on the next page, which summarises the main points.

A Last Word on Obstacles

From reading this book you should be clear about the value of a planned approach, but you may not feel confident about building a detailed plan upfront.

The trick here is to start with whatever level of detail you have, and iterate, iterate, iterate. Something is always better than nothing as a learning tool. When you see reality turn out differently than you assumed, that is a valuable lesson for the future, provided you have some way of including it in your future plans.

Don't be surprised if you need to adjust everyone's expectations along the way — including your own. It takes much more time to deliver change than people realise. The frameworks in this book will give you the tools to set realistic expectations, and thus avoid disappointing others.

Further Support

It's always better to do work like this with the benefit of constructive feedback along the way. I'd be delighted to hear from you if you're thinking about or even doing a scale-up — even if it's just to share your war stories or offer a sympathetic ear for you to bounce an idea off.

If you get started and run aground, I'm here to help. I run one-on-one coaching, workshops, or even hands-on management of change programs. I love helping companies scale up and transform, whatever their industry or state of readiness.

For anything from a short consult to complete intervention, email me here: graeme@pellucid.global. I'll be able to tell you quickly if I can help you in a more organised way. I'll also be direct and tell you if it's beyond my scope, and where else you might want to look for help, if that's the case.

Summary of the 7 Step SCALE WITHOUT FAIL Approach

You & Change	Strategy Compass – Push, Pull, SOAP	Financials	People	Stakeholders	Risk Management	Arrival
STEP 1: Chapter 1	**STEP 2: Chapters 2–4**	**STEP 3: Chapter 5**	**STEP 4: Chapter 6**	**STEP 5: Chapter 7**	**STEP 6: Chapter 8**	**STEP 7: Chapter 9**
Major business change means **major personal change** for you. Test your **motivation** for the scale-up. Understand the difference between steady growth and the scale-up **S-curve**.	Define your **end goal**. Identify and describe your **customers:** their needs will change as you scale up. Quantify **real demand** for your product, test the value you offer. Look closely at your **suppliers** — can you build a reliable business on them, for the right price? Decide whether you should **build or buy.**	Build a **financial plan** that is realistic about timing of outcomes and getting to cash. Test your key **assumptions** — and model your business sensitivity if wrong. Distinguish between **BAU and scale-up costs.**	Be deliberate in how you manage your team: have a **people plan.** Understand your own **strengths and weaknesses** as a leader and manager. Set the **culture** you want your team to follow. Ensure you clearly **communicate** with your team as you scale up.	**Identify** your key stakeholders — owners, enables, potential derailers. Actively manage all major stakeholders — **communicate** with them as much as possible. Make **contingency plans** in case a stakeholder withdraws support.	Understand the **changing risk profile** of your business. Build **upfront risk management initiatives** in your business. Identify all **material risks** and the actions needed to **mitigate** them. Ensure all risks and actions have **lead owners** clearly identified.	Define the key elements of your **target business.** **Signal** to your team when you expect to transition to "steady state". Consider what **extra functional support** your team will need. Define **key operating principles** for your business.

You & Change	Strategy Compass – Push, Pull, SOAP	Financials	People	Stakeholders	Risk Management	Arrival
	Consider your future **competitors** well: learn from them, expect them to react to your success. Identify **constraints** to your scale up and plan how to fix them. Use the 5P framework to build your **SOAP** (strategy on a page). Use the SOAP framework to **quantify and prioritise** your objectives. Use **quantified milestones** to keep your team focused.	Ensure you have allowed for **contingencies** such as errors and unexpected events. Check there are no **"execution cliffs"** in your scale-up plan. **Document your assumptions** and keep good **version control**, so you don't lose track of your **learnings** as you scale up.	Be **consistent** in your messages and management of your team. Expect the scaled-up jobs to **outgrow some of your hires**; deal effectively and promptly with this. Implement strong **people-management practices** early on. Manage your team through the change — create **certainty** of direction and pace for them.	Keep on top of the compliance aspects of the business — **fire prevention**, not firefighting. Get **specialist advice** if needed — and do it early if possible. Keep a **summary** of stakeholder status including actions needed.	Build a **control process** to follow up on mitigating actions. **Review** your risks regularly and often. Make sure you fully understand **legal and regulatory risks.**	**Revise** your own leadership style and approach as needed for a much bigger business. Develop a **continuous-improvement mindset** and embed CAU (change as usual) into your company culture.

And Finally …

Too many people spend their working life doing only what's safe, comfortable and expected of them. If you've read this far, it's because you don't want that to be true of you.

If we had more people like you in business, the world would truly be a better, more productive and more thoughtful place. More exciting, too. That moment when you realise you've crested the first S-curve is amazing. The heavens don't open and choirs don't start singing like in the movies, but it's a feeling I wish everyone could experience. Most of us spend too long working without that satisfaction.

My best wishes to all of you. Follow my approach and the simple steps I've outlined in this book and drive your business to the scale-up success you and your team deserve.

Further Reading

Advisory Board Centre. *Find Out How Advisory Boards are Shaping the Future of Business*. www.advisoryboardcentre.com.au

Christensen, Clayton M. 1997. *The Innovator's Dilemma: When New Technologies Cause Great Firms to Fail*. Boston, MA: Harvard Business School Press, 1997.

Collins, Jim. 2001. *Good to Great: Why Some Companies Make the Leap and Others Don't*. William Collins.

Collins, Jim and Porras, Jerry. 2004. *Built to Last: Successful Habits of Visionary Companies.* Harper Collins.

Covey, Stephen R. 1989. *The Seven Habits of Highly Effective People*. Free Press.

Deloitte Analytics. 2015. *Scale-up: The Experience Game*. Think: School of Creative Leadership. https://www2.deloitte.com/content/dam/Deloitte/nl/Documents/deloitte-analytics/deloitte-nl-data-analytics-onderzoeksrapport-scale-up-the-experience-game.pdf

Drucker, Peter. 1954. *The Practice of Management*. Harper & Row, New York.

Drucker, Peter F. 1946. *Concept of the Corporation.* John Day.

Fractl. n.d. *Decoding Startup Failure: Why 193 Failed Startups Didn't Survive.* https://www.frac.tl/work/marketing-research/why-startups-fail-study/

Goldsmith, Marshall. 2007. *What Got You Here Won't Get You There: How Successful People Become Even More Successful*. Hyperion, United States.

Hamm, John. 2002. "Why Entrepreneurs Don't Scale". Harvard Business Review. https://hbr.org/2002/12/why-entrepreneurs-dont-scale

Harnish, Verne. 2014. *Scaling Up: How a Few Companies Make It ... and Why the Rest Don't.* Gazelles.

Hoffman, Jeff and Finkel, David. 2014. *Scale: Seven Proven Principles to Grow Your Business and Get Your Life Back.* Penguin, New York.

Kahneman, Daniel and Tversky, A. 1981. "The Framing of Decisions and the Psychology of Choice". *Science*, vol. 211, no. 4481. https://psych.hanover.edu/classes/cognition/papers/tversky81.pdf

Korb, A. 2014. "Predictable Fear", *Psychology Today,* https://www.psychologytoday.com/us/blog/prefrontal-nudity/201410/predictable-fear

Kotter, John. 1995. "Leading Change: Why Transformation Efforts Fail". *Harvard Business Review.*

Kruger, Justin and Dunning, David. 2000. "Unskilled and Unaware of It: How Difficulties in Recognizing One's Own Incompetence Lead to Inflated Self-Assessments," *Journal of Personality and Social Psychology*, vol. 77, no. 6.

Kübler-Ross, E. 1969, *On Death and Dying.* Routledge.

Lewin, Kurt. 1947. "Frontiers in Group Dynamics: Concept, Method and Reality in Social Science; Social Equilibria and Social Change". *Human Relations*, June.

Lewis, Michael. 2016. *The Undoing Project.* W.W. Norton. & Company.

McClure, Ben. 2020. "How Venture Capitalists Make Investment Choices". Investopedia.

https://www.investopedia.com/articles/financial-theory/11/how-venture-capitalists-make-investment-choices.asp

Mehrabian, Albert. 1980. *Silent messages: Implicit communication of emotions and attitudes,* Wadsworth.

Moore, Geoffrey A. 1999. *Crossing the Chasm: Marketing and Selling High-Tech Products to Mainstream Customers.* Harper Business.

Peter, Laurence and Hull, Raymond. *1969. The Peter Principle.* William Morrow and Company.

Pellucid Associates. *Does Your Business Need Help to Grow or Reform?* www.pellucid.global

Porter, Michael. 1980. *Competitive Strategy.* Free Press, New York.

Porter, Michael. 1985. *Competitive Advantage.* Free Press, New York.

Taleb, Nassim. 2007. *The Black Swan: The Impact of the Highly Improbable,* Random House.

Yagoda, Ben. 2018. https://www.theatlantic.com/magazine/archive/2018/09/cognit ve-bias/565775/

About the Author

Graeme Hosking is an expert on building, running and transforming large operations. He has worked as a chief operating officer and senior executive in financial services companies around the world. In the mid-1990s, he built and launched the first online banking service for the major UK bank Barclays. During the global financial crisis, he built and ran a global operations team managing payments, international trade and market trading for ANZ's largest customers across 13 countries.

Having worked out how to make "big business" work well, in 2016 he pivoted into a fintech start-up, and from there realised his passion was helping new businesses to grow fast and successfully. He has led scale-up initiatives from pilot to national scale in the UK and Australia and advises a wide range of businesses on their scale-up plans.

He is a mentor for the fintech accelerator hub Stone & Chalk in both Sydney and Melbourne and writes regularly on scale-up and other general business management topics.

Find out more at www.pellucid.global.

www.ingramcontent.com/pod-product-compliance
Lightning Source LLC
Chambersburg PA
CBHW070502200326
41519CB00013B/2679